Contents

The arrangement follows the ancient division of Durham into separ

9th – 13th
w/6

CW00970753

Victorian pillar box
on Palace Green

The Peninsula

The Fortress Site

The historic city of Durham perches precariously on a narrow neck of land below the commanding north wall of the Castle, seat of the bishops whose bishopric stretched from the River Tees to the Scottish Border. East of the old city, an upper reach of the River Wear is crossed by Elvet Bridge, while to the west, Framwellgate Bridge spans a lower stretch. Between these bridges the river flows in a deep gorge almost surrounding the Peninsula whose high, south-sloping plateau is crowned by the great Romanesque Cathedral.

When the Congregation of St Cuthbert arrived in 995, they may have taken the steep route followed by Saddler Street where, in 1974, excavations behind the shops on the west side revealed the remains of a succession of circular wattle buildings with hearths, dating from the 10th century. The Congregation chose the higher site, which could be made impregnable, to settle and build the first church to enshrine the body of their saint. The escarpments and river formed natural defences, the only access being from the north.

The sides of the gorge were originally perpendicular as they remain below St Oswald's, where the ancient burial ground has been respected. Elsewhere, they have been quarried extensively, yielding an estimated 80,000 tons of stone to build the Cathedral, monastic buildings, Castle and fortifications. Geologists calculate that 68,200 tons were needed in the Cathedral itself. The stress on the underlying sandstone is only one-third of the stress which would cause failure.

Early earth and timber fortifications withstood the siege of Malcolm, King of Scots, in 1006. About 1038 his successor, King Duncan, also besieged the site unsuccessfully when citizens sallied forth and slew many Scots.

After the Norman Conquest, William I found a pretext for displacing the Saxon bishop Aegelwine. He was replaced in 1071 by Walcher of Liège (Lorraine), whose friend Waltheof, Earl of Northumberland, was responsible for building the nucleus of the present Castle, although there is evidence of an earlier structure. It became the seat of military, civil and ecclesiastical power from which the bishops of Durham reigned as princes in a buffer state between England and Scotland.

Fortifications

Walls still surrounding the Peninsula augmented the natural defences from an early date. When they were strengthened in the 12th century, an inner wall was erected connecting the Castle keep with the Cathedral choir. The northern entrance at the head of Saddler Street was guarded by a gate-tower with a portcullis. Bishop Langley rebuilt it in 1417 and it became the county prison until 1819. It was demolished in 1820 as an obstruction to carriages.

Parts of the high wall and bastion tower of about 1400 connecting the North Gate and Castle keep are visible near the top of Saddler Street. The street line continues the whole length of the Peninsula in the North and South Baileys, some of whose original houses abutted the outer fortification walls. They were tenanted by bishops' men in return for Castle defence. From Saddler Street, Owengate climbs to Palace Green. A handsome Tudor black and white house stands close to the site of the gate through the inner bailey wall. Nearby in the Castle the bishops' mint issued royal currency.

The Prince-Bishops and their Palace

Palace Green (formerly 'the Place') lies between the Cathedral and the Castle which was also the bishops' palace. Formerly bishops' property within the Castle's outer walls, Palace Green is surrounded by buildings once closely connected with their activities as churchmen, civil administrators and benefactors. Houses covered it until the 12th century, but were removed as pollution risks and fire hazards. Occupants not directly attached to Cathedral or Castle were settled on the site around the present Market Place. When, through the munificence of Bishop and Cathedral Chapter the University was founded, Palace Green was envisaged as its quadrangle. The Castle was handed over to the University, the bishops henceforth using Auckland Castle as their only residence. The University accommodated the episcopal courts, offices and almshouses in new buildings nearby.

The fortress site from the south-west: the Cathedral and monastic buildings to the south rise within the Norman defence walls

The Castle

The Castle gateway, approached across the former dry moat, is Norman; but its exterior was faced in the 18th century by James Wyatt, whose 'restorations' scar both Cathedral and Castle. Massive 16th-century doors, of solid oak and iron, are still closed at night, when the entrance is only by the wicket gate.

Since 1836, Durham Castle has housed University College, the earliest college in Durham University which was founded in 1832. The bishops retain the use of the state apartments and HM judges lodged here during the assizes of 1972.

The Castle began to subside and major restoration work, including piling to stabilise the ground, was undertaken in the 1920s with assistance from the Pilgrim Trust. In 1995 an appeal fund was opened to meet the heavy costs of modern restoration and maintenance.

◁ **Durham Castle courtyard:** west range and Great Hall entrance, with right, the 17th-century turret enclosing the Black Staircase connecting the west and north ranges
➢ **Castle:** Norman chapel
▽ **Castle Gateway** from Palace Green

Courtyard and Norman Chapel

A spacious courtyard is enclosed by buildings of various periods in pleasing harmony. A crypt below the courtyard on the north-east is early Norman. At the lowest level of the east-west range, the Norman undercroft chapel of 1072, originally entered by a newel stair at the south-west, has a nave and two aisles. Plain round pillars of local sandstone with naturally decorative markings support plain groined vaulting. The square abaci of the capitals are carved with grotesque mask-like faces, figures and animals, no two being alike. Part of the herring-bone pavement is probably original. The windows are round-headed; but those on the north, originally 6 inches in width, were widened and the splays increased in 1840. Neglected by later bishops and used as a passage by the early University, it was restored for worship in 1952.

Modern repair and maintenance work in the Castle has been attended by archaeological investigation. Recent discoveries have included an 11th-century oubliette and, in the courtyard, part of the early bishops' lodgings.

The North Range

After a disastrous fire in Silver Street damaged the Castle in the 12th century, Bishop Hugh of Le Puiset built opposite the gateway a lower hall for dining and an upper hall for the constable, responsible for the soldiers, armour and horse of the bishops' army. This, known as the Norman Gallery, was modernised on the outside in the 18th century, but retains window arcades in triplets, with chevron mouldings, inside on the south and west. The matching south-east doorway opens on to a newel stair to the lower hall, which was divided into several rooms by Bishop Tunstal (1530–59). Of these, the bishops' dining-room, now the senior common room, has a contemporary panelled ceiling. The fine senate room fireplace with 17th-century armorials probably originated in the Exchequer.

Bishop Tunstal's Gallery and Chapel

Bishop Tunstal built a gallery on the south front of this lower hall to connect his new chapel on the east with the great hall on the west, destroying the earlier first-floor entrance stair from the courtyard, but leaving the magnificent late Norman doorway in the gallery. The chapel, of 1542, has carved return stalls brought from his chapel at Auckland Castle in 1547, and a 17th-century west screen made for Bishop Cosin whose arms it bears. Bishop Crewe (1674–1721) extended the chapel eastwards but reinstated the original window. The organ in the gallery incorporates some of the pipes and the choir organ case of a 'Father' Smith organ built on the Cathedral screen in 1683, and dismantled in 1872. It was restored in 1921.

The Great Hall

West of the courtyard, a new great hall was built in the late 13th century over the Norman undercroft. Enlarged in about 1350, it had a musicians' gallery and two thrones, one at each end, symbolising the bishop's two roles as prince of church and state. Bishop Fox (1494–1501) reduced the hall to its former length, removing the lower throne and gallery. The two stone pulpits may have been intended for trumpeters.

◄ **The Castle**: Bishop Tunstal's chapel
▼ **Durham Castle: east side of courtyard** with motte surmounted by the rebuilt keep, now containing students' rooms. The adjacent north range contains Tunstal's chapel

Butteries and pantries occupy the space saved; and beyond, a great kitchen, still used, was formed from Bishop Hugh of Le Puiset's south-west tower by inserting windows and three huge fireplaces. The motto *Est Deo Gracia* and the date 1499 are carved on the oak buttery hatch with Bishop Fox's badge, which appears also on the screen between hall and pantries. The device, a 'pelican in her piety' drawing blood from her breast to feed her young, symbolises Christ feeding his Church in the Holy Communion. The present elegant screen and gallery date from 1887. Portraits of University founders and benefactors and the north stained glass window inserted to commemorate its Jubilee are reminders that this is now the dining hall of University College.

The Castle, as church property, was confiscated during the Commonwealth and suffered during ownership by the Lord Mayor of London. After the Restoration in 1660, Bishop Cosin carried out extensive repairs, building the neo-classical portico before the great hall doorway and the tower with the elaborately carved black staircase (1665) at the north end to connect the floors of the Norman wing. The late medieval keep fell into ruin and was replaced by a replica in 1840 to contain undergraduates' rooms.

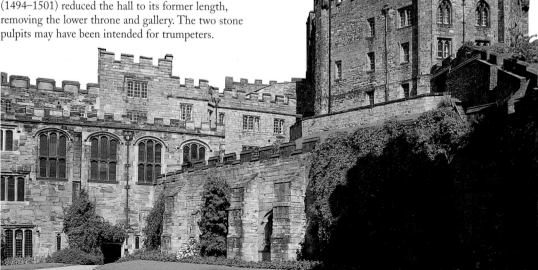

Palace Green

West Side

Leaving the Castle, the wall on the right shelters the Fellows' Garden, once a private retreat for the bishops, adjoining the older University Library buildings which occupy the west side of Palace Green up to Windy Gap, site of the Windishole Postern. The University's main library is at the corner of South Road, in a new building begun in 1982 (*see page 30*).

Nearest the Castle gate, Bishop Neville's Exchequer Building of about 1450 housed various judicial courts. Beneath lierne vaulting and the remains of a newel stair, two doors admit to separate parts of the court room which now contains the Sharp Library of early printed books from Bamburgh Castle. The room above houses Dr Martin Routh's large library of rare books from Magdalen College, Oxford.

Next is the library founded in 1669 by Bishop Cosin for both clergy and the literate public. Its treasures include his annotated copy of *The Book of Common Prayer* of 1611 with suggestions for the revision of 1662. Two original book cases have ends similar to Cosin's chancel stalls. Over the wall cases is a series of portraits of great scholars in groups of three. In 1834 the University added a gallery with a separate entrance by a tower stair from Palace Green for undergraduate use.

The former Diocesan Registry beside Windy Gap was erected in 1820 after the removal of the Assize Courts rebuilt by Bishop Cosin in 1664. Windy Gap leads to the river banks alongside the Dean and Chapter's old Grammar School, built in 1661 and now the University's Music Department. Annexed to it and facing the Cathedral is the former Divinity House, once the residence of J. Meade Faulkner, Cathedral Librarian 1921–32, novelist and author of *The Lost Stradivarius*. The tall cross commemorates Alfred Tucker, appointed Bishop of East Equatorial Africa in 1890 straight from his Durham curacy at St Nicholas.

East Side

Crossing diagonally to the east side of Palace Green, the new Bishop Cosin's almshouses of 1838 stand at the top of Owengate; and the 17th-century house with a magnificent early 18th-century door-head, formerly Archdeacon's Inn, is Bishop Cosin's Hall so-named from use by a University hall of that name between 1851 and 1864. Bishop Cosin's original hospital or almshouse buildings of 1666 are next door. They accommodated four men and four women, as stated in the inscription over the central door:

COSINS HALL

◁ **Palace Green: west side** (left to right) Old Grammar School, Old Registry, University Library (Rare Books), and Bishop Cosin's Library with his coat of arms (top) above the door

▶ **Bishop Cosin's Hall**: 17th-century house with magnificent 18th-century doorhead

Hospitale … pro VIII pauperibus … fundatum 1666.
Schools in the north and south ends were re-foundations of schools of Bishop Langley (1406–37); one taught grammar, with the Latin inscription *Schola pro addiscendis rudimentis literarum*, and the other taught writing and plainsong, with the inscription *Schola pro plano canto et arte scribendi*. The University built new accommodation for the alms people at the head of Owengate and converted the earlier buildings to lecture rooms (later linked with the adjoining neo-gothic Pemberton building). They are now the Almshouse Café and Restaurant.

On the corner, Abbey House with its Queen Anne front earlier faced south. Its ancient blocked doorway is close to the site of another gate in the inner bailey wall at the head of Lygate (*lich* – corpse) beside the Cathedral graveyard. Lygate was re-named Dun Cow Lane after the 18th-century renewal of the carving, high on the Cathedral's north face. It represents the legend, first recorded in the late 16th century, of a woman calling her dun cow directing the Congregation of St Cuthbert to the Peninsula.

⌃ **Dun Cow Lane** leading from North Bailey to Palace Green

▶ **Dun Cow Lane: ancient blocked doorway to Abbey House** (the Queen Anne front now faces Palace Green)

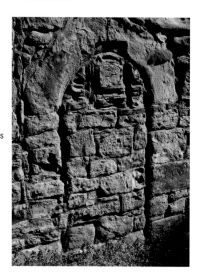

The Cathedral

St Cuthbert

The young St Cuthbert, noble and attractive, saw a vision on the night of St Aidan's death in 652 and the next day went to Melrose to enter its monastery. Soon, moving to Ripon, he became guest-master but, with Celtic training, fell foul of Wilfred and Roman practices. Returning to Melrose he became Prior, was transferred to Lindisfarne (Holy Island) in 664 and became Bishop in 684. He died in 687 on his beloved island of Inner Farne and was buried in Lindisfarne Priory. His stone coffin was opened twelve years later, revealing his body fresh as in life. A miracle was proclaimed and the body, transferred to an oak casket, was venerated.

Flight from Holy Island

In danger from Danish raiders, the Congregation of St Cuthbert, descendants of the earlier community, left Lindisfarne in 875 and, with their wives, children and cattle, began their 'wanderings' over the north. Among the treasures they took with them was an elaborately carved oak casket which had two partitions. In the lower portion lay St Cuthbert's body with the bones of St Aidan and other saints, and St Oswald's head. The upper part held valuable manuscripts, including the Lindisfarne Gospels now in the British Museum, and the related Durham Gospels, still in Durham. The Congregation with its bishop settled at Chester-le-Street in 882; but further danger in 995 sent them to Ripon and finally to Durham.

Here they built a temporary wooden shrine, south of the present Cathedral, to protect their treasures, followed by a 'White Church' of stone with east and west towers and a shrine for St Cuthbert's relics. The graves of the early Congregation, men, women and children, were found during 19th-century restoration of the chapter house and four of the cross-heads discovered with them are on display.

Perhaps for political reasons, as their lands were hereditary, the Congregation of St Cuthbert was ejected under William I. Bishop Walcher of Lorraine (1071–80) planned monastic buildings, traces of which are incorporated in the south-east corner of the cloister and include a wide branched staircase, now broken, leading to the early dormitory, and the deanery and refectory undercrofts. The introduction of celibate Benedictine monks led to the growth of the legend that St Cuthbert disliked women.

The Present Church

In 1093, Bishop Walcher's successor, Bishop William of St Calais or Carilef (1081–96) demolished the 'White Church' to build a new Cathedral with its south wall 30 ft north of the north wall of its predecessor. It had apsidal (rounded) ends to choir and aisles in the manner inspired during his exile in Normandy during 1088–91. An architectural adventure, this is the earliest example in

The Galilee

After an attempt to add an eastern chapel, unsuccessful because of unstable ground, Bishop Hugh of Le Puiset (1153–95) added the Galilee to the west end in about 1175. This chapel covered the Cathedral's western forecourt and severed the double fortification wall to the south (still intact) from the wall-passage running north to the Castle. Its well, rediscovered in March 1896, had an outer dip-well for public use (*see page 25*) whose overflow later formed St Cuthbert's Well on the banks below.

The Galilee roof is supported by slender Purbeck marble pillars augmented by stone columns. In 1414, Bishop Langley added his chantry and altar tomb during his lifetime, blocking the great west door and providing two side doors to the nave.

The alcove to the north contained the Holy Cross altar where 12th-century wall-paintings of a bishop and a knight flanking looped curtains are probably associated with Bishop Hugh of Le Puiset as builder of the Galilee and with the donor of the relics of the cross once displayed in a central niche, now blocked behind the modern cross. Nineteenth-century writers identified them with St Cuthbert and St Oswald. To the south is the tomb of the Venerable Bede. His bones were brought from Jarrow to Durham by Aelfred the Sacrist about 1022 and transferred from the feretory (behind the high altar) to the Galilee in 1366–7.

Ancient Sanctuary

After the Galilee was built, the north door of the nave became the Cathedral's main entrance. Internally this doorway remains as it was built in the time of Bishop Geoffrey Rufus (1133–40) with its outer arch ornamented by foliage and eighteen diamond-shaped medallions, some depicting animals or birds, others illustrating lively scenes from real life or legend: a man whips a boy lying over a stool while holding up his dress; two people embrace; a long-robed and bearded man with a rope strangles another wearing a knee-length garment;

north-west Europe of a church planned to be roofed entirely by stone-ribbed vaulting. By 1104 the eastern end was finished except for the north transept, which was vaulted in 1110. Under Bishop Rannulf Flambard (1099–1128) the nave was completed except for the vaulting, which the monks achieved during the next five years when the see was vacant. The main church was finished in 1133. The compound piers of the nave alternate with circular columns, whose girth equals the height from base to capital (22 ft), in matching pairs of chevron, diaper and spiral designs, deeply incised. The massive stones, quarried locally, were brought to the church carved ready for erection. The style of the wall-arcading of interlaced arches was probably first used in Durham, while the transverse arches supporting the nave vaulting are probably the earliest pointed arches in England. The interior was painted with brilliant colours and designs, of which a restored example may be seen on the south wall of the nave.

⌃ **View from Cathedral Central tower** looking towards the Western Towers and across the river to South Street

⌄ **Sanctuary Knocker** on Cathedral's North Door (really a closing ring, but used as a knocker by fugitives seeking sanctuary)

► **Cathedral east end**

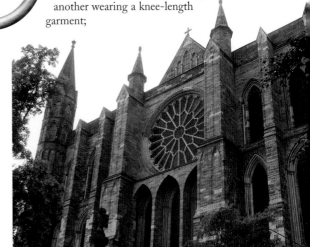

two show centaurs with conical helmets shooting with bows and arrows.

When this doorway was created it was entered through a stately porch (later enhanced by buttresses). From two chambers above, reached by stairs descending from the triforium, monks kept watch day and night for fugitives seeking sanctuary, who grasped and knocked with the ring in the mouth of the bronze lion's head on the door below. Enamelled or glazed eyes must once have emphasised its grotesque appearance. The sanctuary seeker was admitted immediately and the Galilee bell rung in the north-west tower.

He was allowed 37 days' refuge, with food, drink and bedding, in a grated enclosure beneath the dormitory night stairs between the south door and the Galilee door. Clad in a black cloth gown, with St Cuthbert's cross in yellow on the left shoulder, he was safe within the sanctuary of church and churchyard until he received royal pardon, or came to terms with his accusers. If neither happened he was required to forfeit his goods and renounce the realm, walking in his distinctive robe to the nearest port carrying a wooden cross. Three hundred and thirty-one men claimed the sanctuary of St Cuthbert between 1464 and 1524, and the privilege continued until James I's reign.

The outer porch, with its chambers above, was demolished by James Wyatt, who reduced the doorway to its present appearance with the outer decoration shaved off and re-carved.

The original 12th-century 'sanctuary knocker' suffered corrosion caused by industrial fall-out pollution. It was removed for conservation at the British Museum where a bronze replica was cast and in 1980 replaced the original, which is now displayed in the Treasury.

Chapel of the Nine Altars

In the 13th century, with improved building techniques, the Nine Altars' chapel was achieved at the east end. (As Benedictine monks were ordained priests, each celebrating mass daily, many altars were needed.) In its north transept a statue of Bishop William Van Mildert (1826–36) commemorates the last count-palatine, co-founder of the University and donor of the Castle.

The Shrine

From the Nine Altars' chapel, steps lead to a raised platform behind the high altar. Here was the medieval feretory, where relics were kept. In the centre stood the richly decorated shrine of St Cuthbert, visited by innumerable pilgrims. Its treasures were removed by Henry VIII's commissioners in 1537. Today the saint's remains lie beneath a simple inscribed slab marked by four tall candlesticks, designed by Sir Ninian Comper, as was the tester, depicting Christ in Glory surrounded by the symbols of the four Evangelists. It hangs from the four holes in the vault above from which once hung the painted and gilded shrine cover. A semi-circular white line shows the site of the apse, the original east end of the Norman church.

The Choir

The delicate altar screen, partly paid for by John, Lord Neville, between 1372 and 1380, was brought from Caen in Normandy. The bishop's throne, the highest in Christendom, was erected by Bishop Hatfield (1345–81) above his tomb with its many coats of arms. Scottish royalist soldiers' imprisoned in the Cathedral after their defeat by Cromwell at the Battle of Dunbar in 1640, destroyed the woodwork except for the elaborate clock of about 1500 in the south transept. Bishop Cosin inspired the style of the pinnacled choir stalls which replaced the lost medieval stalls in 1665. Their return stalls and matching screen, with its 'Father' Smith organ built in 1683, were removed when Sir Gilbert Scott designed the present screen (1870–6). The west face of the 17th-century screen, partly reconstructed in the south-west aisle, is markedly different in style; and matching choir aisle doors have been re-used to lead to the Castle buttery. The early (romanesque) screen was solid stone; two of its rescued sculptured panels, which had been re-used as building material, are displayed in the Treasury.

Cloister, Precincts and Library

The remains of the medieval Benedictine monastery to the south of the church are the most complete in England. The cloister garth, surrounded by alleys once protected by glazed windows, has its well and the basin from the monks' lavatorium (washing place) which formerly stood opposite the refectory door.

▶ **Cathedral: the choir and nave looking west**
◀ **Cloisters; the western alley**, with monks' dormitory above

The north alley, against the church, enclosed part of the monastic library and study alcoves. On the eastern alley is the chapter house, completed by Bishop Rufus (1133–40), containing the graves of early bishops. Above the slype or passage connecting it with the south transept Prior John Wessington (1416–46) built a room to which he moved the library from the cloister. South of the cloister the Norman refectory, derelict after the dissolution and temporary use as a petty canons' hall, was converted by Dean Sudbury, about 1684, into the Dean and Chapter Library. In 1854 the immense dormitory, built 1396-1404 and spanned by complete oak trees, was added to the library. The library contains over 50,000 volumes including about 360 volumes of medieval manuscripts, some of Bede's time from Jarrow and Wearmouth.

The Great Kitchen

The old doorway next to the refectory entrance has been re-opened to give access to the vast octagonal kitchen built in the 14th century by the master mason John Lewin. It has six great fireplaces and intricate vaulting to support a central louvre to expel fumes. After monastic times, it served as the kitchen for the Deanery until 1940 and was connected with it by a long rising passage (since demolished) built against the south wall of the refectory. Later it housed thousands of Priory and Cathedral documents dating from the 11th century onwards, and administered in co-operation with the University. In 1992 they were moved to No. 5, The College, making it possible to use the Great Kitchen as the Cathedral bookshop from 1997.

Undercrofts and Treasury

There is now a restaurant beneath the dormitory in the south end of the undercroft, formerly cellars for the adjacent great kitchen, while the north part, once the monk's common room, is now the Treasury. Here St

▲ **Sundial** on the south face of the Great Kitchen
► **The Great Kitchen:** interior with vaulting (now the Cathedral Bookshop)
↗ **The Great Kitchen:** east side, with offices beside the Durham Light Infantry memorial garden in the College

Cuthbert's 'coffin', portable altar and cross, with Anglo-Saxon embroidery, manuscripts and other treasures are displayed for visitors.

From the south-east corner of the cloister a passage, probably constructed in the 17th century, leads to the College or Cathedral Close. Within the passage, opposite doors lead to two exhibitions: in the refectory undercroft (right) built *c.* 1080, is now *Building the church*, an imaginative display designed for school children (access by appointment only); the contemporary undercroft to the Prior's Hall (left) houses *Cuthbert yesterday and today: an audio-visual of the living Cathedral* (18 minutes), with superb photography. (For opening hours, which vary according to season, see the notice board at north door of the Cathedral.)

The College (Cathedral Close)

Continue down the passage to the College. During the Commonwealth, Oliver Cromwell arranged to found a university here. Staff were appointed but no students were enrolled.

The Deanery abuts the refectory and incorporates 11th-century work and the medieval priors' hall. Opposite is the Durham Light Infantry memorial garden, sheltered by the refectory's south wall and the octagonal 14th-century Great Kitchen.

The steep 'dark entry' leads west to the river banks beneath the sub-dean's house where the early Norman vaulted undercroft of the guest-house survives. Adjacent houses, set back, surmount of St John's College, re-furbished in 2002. Although partly rebuilt in 1846 by G.R. Pickering , when the Reverend James Raine was Rector (*see also page 18*), it contains Norman work, an oval stone relief of Christ seated in glory and surrounded by symbols of the four evangelists of about 1215, brought from St Giles in the north wall of the chancel, a foliated tomb lid built into the south wall of the chancel, coloured historic heads as roof bosses, and 17th-century woodwork. The stained glass windows are mostly by Wailes. Many distinguished parishioners were buried here. Near the organ is a wall memorial to the dwarf 'Count' Boruwlaski whose grave is in the Cathedral near the north-western tower, and who lived latterly in a house, since demolished, just outside the Water Gate.

The south sanctuary window contains the coat of arms of the Bowes family of Bradley Hall, ancestors of the Queen, two of whose members are buried in the chancel floor and another in the churchyard. Their town house stands opposite the church. The bailey houses gradually became gentlemen's town residences with gardens stretching to the east bailey wall and below to the river. 'Bowes House', 4, South Bailey, now part of St John's College, is typical of these. The late Queen Mother enjoyed visits here. Occupants and history can be traced from medieval times. Owned in 1452 by the Master of Kepier Hospital, it had access to the monastic

the infirmary undercroft, while Georgian-style houses to the south are conversions from monastic outbuildings. The 18th-century tower was a reservoir for water, piped across the river from medieval times.

Beside the gateway of *c.* 1500 is a medieval lane spanned by an early timber-framed granary, leading to the gylehouse (where gyle or wort, an infusion of malt, was fermented to make beer), brewhouse and bakehouse.

South Bailey

Just outside the gates was the monastery's almonry school whose Master, also Master of St Mary Magdalene Hospital, controlled the almonry where the children slept and four old women lived (24, North Bailey). In the other direction the South Bailey had its own parish church of St Mary-the-Less, now the chapel

⌖ **Water tower** controlling water piped from springs across the river

⌖ **Water pump** once used communally by canons' houses

▸ **St Mary-the-Less:** south side

▸▸ **St Mary-the-Less:** armorial window to the Bowes family

cellarers' orchard beyond the wall.
Later occupants included the widow
of Dean Whittingham, translator of
the Geneva Bible (quoted by
Shakespeare), the Bowes family in the
17th and 18th centuries, the Liddells
(whose descendant inspired *Alice in
Wonderland*) and many famous
clergy. The reception room has a
delicate 18th-century plaster ceiling.
South Bailey descends to the Water
Gate which superseded the medieval
gate in 1778. The wall on the right
retains its sentry walk, while on the
left, guard towers stand sentinel at intervals to
Kingsgate. St John's College main building, once a
private house, built about 1730, has an imposing
doorway up a broad flight of steps (*see page 29*) and a
fine staircase. The College has extended into adjacent
houses.

North Bailey

Returning to the North Bailey, some houses are
reputedly haunted: an elegant lady and almonry children
(no. 23), a musician (no. 24), and a crooked man in black
breeches, ruffled shirt and nightcap emerging from a
cellar.

St Chad's College, on the corner of Bow Lane, faces
the Cathedral. Part of its hall, built in 1961, replaced
a quaint bow-windowed house where the gifted Porter
family lived before leaving for Edinburgh in 1780.
Jane (1776–1850) wrote *The Scottish Chiefs* (1810), a
novel with Durham references; Robert (1777–1842)
became Sir Robert Ker Porter, author and painter of
historical panoramas, and married a Russian princess;
and Anna Maria (1780–1832) published *Artless Tales*
in 1793. Prince Leopold read her *Knight of St John* to
Princess Charlotte on the eve of her death (1817).

Bow Lane leads to the site of the Kingsgate postern
and ford, traditionally associated with William the
Conqueror's flight. Supposedly, he was seized with dread
after an attempted opening of St Cuthbert's coffin to
challenge the belief that the body was incorrupt,
mounted his horse and galloped, non-stop, terrified to
draw rein until over the Tees into Yorkshire and safe
from the saint's power. In the 15th century Bow Bridge
crossed the river here. Today the Kingsgate footbridge
leads to Dunelm House and Elvet; and steps, formerly a
grassy vennel, descending to the riverside path,
emphasise the impregnability of the strong walls above
the steep slopes. Bow Lane has views of Hatfield
College whose main gates and chapel (1853) are in
North Bailey, and the fine 18th-century house with
handsome portico and panelled interior. The College
nucleus is the mid-18th-century 'Red Lion' coaching
inn, whose elegant dining-room, once assembly rooms,
has a Venetian window. In 1827 Durham had about 18
daily coaches and 41 carriers before railways caused the

◄ **St Mary-the-Less: nave roof corbel** of Norman
head in chain mail
▼ **Bow Lane** descends from North Bailey to the
river. The porte-cochère on the right spanning the
pavement before the 18th-century house protected
ladies alighting from carriages before the invention
of umbrellas

business to decline. Alongside the lane,
St Mary-le-Bow's south wall was part of
the inner bailey wall whose gateway (or
'bow') crossing North Bailey, was
annexed to the church. Both fell in 1637.
Church rebuilding was completed in
1685 and the tower in *c.* 1702. Within is good
contemporary woodwork. Closed in 1967, it was
converted to a heritage centre in 1976.

The cottage next the churchyard hides timber-
framing; and north of Hatfield College gates is 'Jevons'
which replaces the Georgian house of John Gulley
(1783–1863), champion prize-fighter of England in
1806. On the left, Bailey House covers the site of a
maison dieu (where medieval pilgrims could lodge),
and Museum Square up to Dons' Passage. On Owengate
corner the University's Law Department occupies the
former Halmote Court office (closed in 1952). After its
removal from Palace Green in 1855, Durham's Chancery
Court continued to function here and contained the
judicial seat from the bishops' Exchequer Building.

Borough of Durham and Framwellgate

The borough of Durham, below the north walls of the Castle, was one of six separately administered areas (the boroughs of Durham, Crossgate, Gilligate, Elvet borough, Elvet barony and St Mary Magdalene) now within the modern city. It comprised only the Market Place, Saddler Street and Silver Street with the addition of the suburbs of Claypath and Framwellgate from an early date.

Saddler Street

Saddler Street descends steeply from the Peninsula to the Market Place. After the demolition of the North Gate at the street head in 1820, a subscription library and assembly rooms were built. The latter, now the Salvation Army Citadel, has fluted pillars similar to those of the two shop-fronts beside Drury Lane lower down. Across this vennel, so-called by 1754, the former robe-maker's shop masks the foyer of an 18th-century theatre whose auditorium sloped down to a stage below. The street had several theatres, including two opposite, opened in 1771 and 1791. Here, Stephen Kemble engaged actors such as his sister Mrs Siddons (1755–1831).

The street between Magdalene Steps (leading to Elvet Bridge) and the Market Place was formerly named Fleshergate in living memory, and occupied by butchers (flesh-hewers). Mrs Clemens' famous Durham mustard was probably first ground at a mill behind no.73 in the 17th century. The business descended to Ainsleys and was bought by Colman's c.1900.

The street retains a number of Tudor properties. The best example of a merchant's house is no.79. The timber-framed structure and attic fireplace may be 14th-century and a fine 17th-century staircase connects the four storeys. 'Neptune' heads, roses, fleurs-de-lys, pomegranates and thistles decorate its elaborate and priceless second-floor plaster ceiling of about 1560.

Elvet Bridge

Magdalene Steps lead from Fleshergate (used as the shambles until the 19th century) to Elvet Bridge. Approximately two-thirds of the bridge is in St Nicholas parish, the remainder being in Elvet. A slab of blue marble formerly marked the boundary between the two. (*See page 24, column 2, for an account of St Andrew's chapel at the Elvet end of the bridge.*)

The bridge has ten arches (fourteen according to Leland in the 16th century) and was built by Bishop Hugh of Le Puiset (1153–95), reconstructed *c.* 1228, repaired extensively under Bishop Fox (1494–1501) and again in 1601. Before 1400, shops and houses were built on the ends of the bridge, and the spaces under the dry or land arches were leased out for storage. The great flood of 1771 destroyed three arches, but refuges (alcoves for pedestrian safety) remained until 1804–5 when the bridge's width was doubled and the low vennel (formerly reached down steps from the Market Place) on the north-west was covered.

A medieval gate formerly pierced the city wall, the remains of which are now hidden by shops in the former Souterpeth (shoemakers' street). The mayor met James I in 1617 at the north-west bridge tower beside the 13th-century St James' chapel, founded by Lewin, a Durham burgess. Both tower and chapel have long vanished.

Bastion tower base, part of the outer defences of the Castle

Saddler Street on Miners' Gala Day. A miners' lodge banner passes Magdalene Steps in the procession to the old race course

Saddler Street with Tudor houses looking toward the Market Place

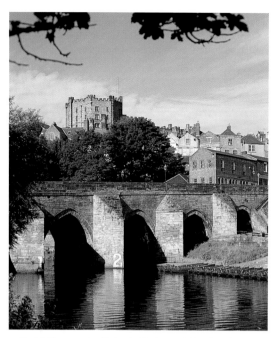

▲ **Elvet Bridge**, once fortified at the Durham end, rises from Elvet towards the Market Place

▼ **Market Place and St Nicholas' church on market day:** equestrian statue of of the 3rd Marquess of Londonderry in hussar uniform – the finest work of Raffaelle Monti (1818–81), executed for Durham in 1858 and erected 1861. The Town Hall is in the left background

The chapel was replaced in 1632 by the House of Correction. Its former workhouse, repaired in 1715 to be used with the woollen manufactory in the Market Place, is part of the shop next to the post-1820 archway on the south side of the bridge and two floors below the modern street level. The House of Correction and its workhouse were connected by a passage bridging the old low vennel, with steps descending from a high doorway in the bridge arch which is now visible. A lower doorway leads to the two cells remaining below the bridge on the north side. Here, Jimmy Allen, champion of the Northumbrian pipes and piper to the Duchess of Northumberland, was imprisoned for horse-stealing. Pardon came the day after his death. His ghostly piping is said to haunt the cells remaining beneath the bridge. Other cells remain beneath adjacent shops.

The Market Place

From the Market Place, Silver Street, now pedestrianised, descends westwards to Framwellgate Bridge and the suburbs of Framwellgate and Crossgate; while Claypath leads north-east to Gilesgate from the east end of St Nicholas' church. Here stood the Clayport Gate, demolished in 1791, which passed through walls running east and west beside Paradise Lane and Walkergate (both destroyed) which connected fords of the Wear just south of the modern Leazes Road roundabout and Millburngate Bridge.

Remains of these walls, built about 1314 by the burgesses after Scottish raids, lie beneath shops on the east side of the Market Place.

The medieval Market Place, where a weekly Saturday market still flourishes, was dominated by St Nicholas' church with its churchyard, the Tolbooth, and the Pant. It was extended *c.* 1841 by the paving of St Nicholas' churchyard where the Tanners' Guild traded.

Guilds affiliated to the 15th-century Corpus Christi Guild, whose guildhall stood behind Claypath, once controlled trade and commerce and linger on today. Market tolls were collected in the Tollbooth, where the bishops' bailiff held a fortnightly court in a room above shops and stalls, until Bishop Tunstal built a stone Guildhall on the west side of the Market Place. In his time the marble sanctuary cross from Gilesgate was moved here. This was replaced for James I's visit in 1617 by one with a lead roof and twelve-pillared arcade, subsequently demolished. Its stone was used to build a nine-arched piazza south of St Nicholas' churchyard in 1780.

The Pant provided the only public well from 1450, with water piped across the river to supply Bacon Place, on the east side of the Market Place, the town house of Thomas Billingham of Crook Hall. The well-head, surmounted from 1729 by Neptune, renewed in 1863 and 1900, remained until 1920. The statue of Neptune was removed to Wharton Park (above the railway station) but was badly damaged there. It was repaired and refurbished to grace the Market Place again from May 1991. Neptune is associated with an 18th-century scheme, never implemented, to make the Wear navigable up-river as far as Durham, to promote industry and commerce.

Town Hall and Guildhall

An equestrian statue of the 3rd Marquess of Londonderry (*see picture opposite*), in hussar uniform, stands in front of the Town Hall steps. It is the finest work of Raffaelle Monti (1818–81).

When the city's business outgrew the old Guildhall, a new Town Hall was erected to the rear and opened on 29 January 1851. In the 60-foot long entrance corridor is a copy of Bishop Hugh of Le Puiset's charter to the burgesses in 1179. The original is preserved in the County Record Office with those of Bishop Pilkington (1565), Bishop Matthew (1602), Bishop Crewe (1685) and Bishop Egerton (1780). Bishop Crewe gave most of the present civic plate, hallmarked 1672–95, as the corporation had misappropriated its early silver.

Showcases contain the clothes and violin of 'Count' Boruwlaski, a Polish dwarf 39 inches tall, who published his *Memoirs* and musical compositions. After extensive travels he came to England in 1782. He spent the last years of his life in Durham and was a friend of the Ebdons. Thomas Ebdon, the composer, was Cathedral organist from 1763 until his death in 1811. (He is remembered today for some of his church music, and especially for the evening canticles of his Service in C.) The Misses Ebdon kept house for Boruwlaski at a cottage, now demolished, below 12, South Bailey, near Count's Corner where he died in 1837 in his late nineties. (*See also page 26.*)

The Town Hall, 72 feet long and 36 feet wide, was designed by P. C. Hardwicke of London with a fine hammer-beam roof, 56 feet to the ridge, to imitate that of Westminster Hall, a reminder that the ancient bishops' courts were modelled on those of Westminster.

The decor represents the city's history. Twelve angels terminating the roof beams, and shields within the quatrefoils in the spandrels of the arched beams, display the coats of arms of its sixteen incorporated trade guilds. Over the Prudhoe stone fireplace are the arms of Bishop Maltby (1835–56) impaled with those of the see; and flanking panels record the men who fell in World War I (1914–18), and the city's honorary freemen. High wainscoting bears the names and dates of mayors, chaplains and town clerks since the 1835 Municipal Corporation Act, when the bishops' Palatinate jurisdiction was transferred to the Crown. The coats of arms of leading county families embellish the upper walls and panels below the west window. Its top lights

Town Hall west window illustrating scenes from the city's history

display the arms of Allan of Blackwell, Shipperdson of Durham, Wharton of Dryburn, and the architect; side lights represent bishops who gave charters to the city: Hugh of Le Puiset, James Pilkington, Tobias Matthew and Nathaniel Crewe; the lowest panels show Edward III, with his barons, thanking the citizens for their loyalty; and three central lights depict the medieval guilds' annual procession to the Cathedral on Corpus Christi day bearing banners and torches, as they were affiliated to the Corpus Christi guild founded by Bishop Langley (1406–37). Their mystery plays are lost, but fine guild silver survives, and some guild records, including the Dyers and Litzters Book, are preserved.

The Guildhall (left of the entrance corridor) was built by Bishop Tunstal in 1535 to replace one associated with St Nicholas in 1316. After damage during the 1640 Scottish invasion, Bishop Cosin rebuilt it in 1665. Major alterations in 1752 were soon followed by re-facing and possibly rebuilding; but the oak fittings and carved coats of arms are Cosin's. On the walls hang guild coats of arms, painted in 1783–85. One represents the Merchant Company (1561) comprising Grocers (1345), Mercers (1393), Salters (1394), Ironmongers (1464), and Haberdashers (1487). Ten others represent the Cordwainers, workers in Cordova leather or shoemakers (1430); Skinners (1327) joined by the Glovers (1638); Weavers (1450); Drapers and Tailors (1549); Butchers (1520); Blacksmiths, Lorrimers (makers of spurs and bits), Locksmiths, Cutlers and Bladesmiths (1610); Free Masons, Rough Masons, Wallers, Slaters, Paviours, Plaisterers and Bricklayers (1410-11); Carpenters, Joiners, Coopers, Wheelwrights and Sawyers (1571); Barber-Chirurgeons, Ropers and Stringers (1468); and Goldsmiths, Plumbers, Pewterers, Potters, Painters and Glaziers (1532). The Dyers became extinct in 1811 when the last member died. These guilds played an important part in civic life until 1835, when their principal rights were removed. Several surviving guilds still meet here.

The adjacent Mayor's Chamber was panelled by George Bowes MP in 1752, doubled in size in 1848–49 and was altered in 1890. Its magnificent fireplace was presented by Walter Scruton, Clerk of the Peace, when he sold the building that is now Hatfield College to the University . He took out the fireplace, but removed from the over-mantel portraits of Charles I and Queen Henrietta Maria, now replaced by reproductions.

The Burlison Art Gallery, right of the corridor, and above part of the Market Hall, is named after its chief benefactor, Clement Burlison (1830–99), a local landscape painter.

This is the site of New Place, town residence of the Nevilles of Raby and Earls of Westmorland, whose gardens sloped down to the river. The Crown confiscated the property in 1569 after the rebellion of the northern earls. Henry Smith's charity bought it from James II for use as a school, cloth manufactory and St Nicholas' parish workhouse. The buildings were demolished in 1852 and rebuilt as they stand today. In 1926 Durham Corporation bought the whole site, including that of the Town Hall.

Framwellgate Bridge from the riverside path below South Street

St Nicholas' Church

In 1283 Archbishop Wickwane fled down steps at the west end of St Nicholas' church to Kepier Hospital after a rebellious reception at Durham Priory.

St Nicholas' church, whose Norman north wall once continued the city wall, became unsafe after alterations. It was rebuilt in 1858 to a neo-gothic design by J. F. Pritchett. *Jesu, lover of my soul* was first sung to J. B. Dykes' well-known tune at the re-opening. The church was modernised in 1981.

Opposite, the Prince-Bishops shopping precinct leads from the east side of the Market Place to the head of Elvet Bridge.

Claypath

Much of the ancient Claypath has vanished. To the left, at the foot of the former Walkergate (or cloth-workers' street) stood Henderson's factory which succeeded the woollen industry of St Nicholas' workhouse. William Henderson demolished Shakelock Hall (which superseded an earlier mansion) c. 1840 to extend his works. Hugh Mackays, makers of the famous Durham carpets, followed Henderson and recently moved their factory to Meadowfield Industrial Estate on the south-western outskirts. The site north of St Nicholas' church and the sliproad have been developed to form Millenium Place, with the Clayport Library (County Branch Library, so-called because near the site of the Clayport Gate), Gala Theatre and Tourist Information Centre. The nearby car and coach park is essential as the centre of Durham, from the foot of Claypath, including the Market Place and Silver Street, to the west end of Framwellgate Bridge, is closed to vehicular traffic, except for a bus which carries passengers up Saddler Street to Palace Green for the Cathedral and Castle, and to and from the railway station. For those on foot, the modern Pennyferry Bridge named from a former penny ferry, connects with Framwellgate waterside.

On the east side of Claypath behind shops is the neglected Quaker burial ground and the site of the Bluecoat School. Opposite, the Independent Chapel of 1751 is hidden behind the neo-gothic Congregational church of c.1888, the United Reformed church until 2003.

Leazes Place, in Regency style, was built, surprisingly, in 1843–6. It leads to Leazes House, erected for William Henderson c. 1847, which Durham High School held 1887–1968 and then Durham University owned, but is now divided into flats.

Providence Row, next to the former General Post Office (now flats), leads to the riverside. Here the Sands, greensward stretching to Kepier Hospital, is the Freemen's common pasture and the site of a traditional Holy Week fair. On the slope above, St Nicholas' 'new' churchyard adjoins the site of St Thomas' chapel, whose burial ground, approached by a lane from Claypath, was used as late as the plague year of 1597. Near the Sands, below Millburngate Bridge, the burgesses ground their corn at the Bishop's Mill, recorded in Boldon Book (1183), rebuilt in the 17th century and demolished in 1972. The mill race later served an adjacent ice rink. Between this and the site of the Clock Mill, opposite, the dam and weir deepen the water, providing extra defence for the Castle.

Returning to Claypath, Bakehouse Lane, site of a medieval common bakehouse, leads to Mayorswell field, named from the Maire family, former owners. Robert and Grace Maire became Roman Catholics after seeing men of that faith hanged at Gibbet Knowle, Dryburn, in 1591.

Tinklers' Passage, opposite, leading towards the river, formed the boundary of St Nicholas' parish, once marked also by a medieval leaden cross standing in the roadway. From here, Gilesgate rises to a modern roundabout and beyond it, Gilesgate Green, centre of a formerly separate settlement with its parish church of St Giles (*see p.20*).

Silver Street and Framwellgate Bridge

Silver Street, descending to Framwellgate Bridge, is now pedestrianised. Of its former timber-framed houses only three remain, two on the north side. When in 1964 the fine house of Sir John Duck (*d*.1691) was demolished, its black oak staircase was rescued by Bowes Museum, Barnard Castle, and a panel painting depicting Duck's story was saved by Alderman Luke. When Duck was an unemployed butcher's apprentice, a raven dropped a gold sovereign at his feet and his fortune changed. He became master-butcher, mayor, keel, ship and mine owner, founder of Lumley almshouses and Sir John Duck of Haswell-on-the-Hill.

Two steep vennels or alleys join Moatside Lane which skirts the Castle motte. A medieval maison dieu, or hospice for pilgrims, existed on a site above the lower vennel until the 17th century.

Bishop Rannulf Flambard, whose competence as William II's tax collector gained him the bishopric, built Framwellgate Bridge about 1120. After damage by flood in 1401, it was rebuilt using tolls from a temporary ferry and money from the Prior and Convent and Bishop Langley (1406–37). The Castle's Norman gallery immediately overlooks it; towers and gates defended each end and a postern led to the river banks. Increasing traffic led to the removal of the Silver Street gate in 1760 and the battlements in 1828, and bridge widening in the early 19th century. (*See also the Banks, page 25.*)

Framwellgate

Across the bridge, Crossgate lies to the left and Framwellgate to the right. The boundary between was the Mill Burn, now in a conduit beneath North Road, which was opened as King Street in 1831, William IV's coronation year.

Framwellgate was reached formerly through Millburngate, which survives only as a footway beside a timber-framed house at the entrance to Millburngate shopping centre. Here, steps descend to the riverside near the site of two mills, where the Mill Burn cascades from a pipe into the river beside the weir. A path joins the road beneath Millburngate Bridge and beside Millburngate House (modern government buildings) to Crook Hall, which may be reached also via Framwellgate and Sidegate.

The prosperous merchants' houses of Framwellgate became 19th-century slums and were demolished, except for an

Millennium Place and Gala Theatre seen from Millburngate Bridge

18th-century town house with beautiful plasterwork *c.* 1741. Today, it overlooks Millburngate roundabout. Once the Wheatsheaf Inn, it became a convent, later an arts centre, and is now let as flats.

Beside it, ancient Castle Chare, now a modern road, climbs steeply to the railway station past St Godric's Roman Catholic church, built for Irish workers who moved here in the 19th century. It was restored after serious fire damage in 1984.

Crook Hall and Sidegate

Crook Hall (a private house) overlooks the river where waterside steps led to a ferry to the Sands within living memory. The boat was worked from a cable across the river.

The site, occupied before 1217, was part of the manor of Sidegate. The 14th-century manor house was probably built by Peter del Croke. The solar wing is ruined, but the hall, open to the roof, survives with minstrels' gallery and screens passage. Here lived Joan del Croke, who married John de Copeland. He captured King David of Scotland at Beau Repaire (Bearpark) when northern armies routed the Scots at the Battle of Neville's Cross in 1346, afterwards being knighted and made constable of Roxburgh. He and Joan held Crook Hall until 1362 when he became Keeper of Berwick.

The Billinghams lived here *c.* 1390–1667, altering the west end and creating from the earlier buttery and pantry a winter parlour whose timbers were decorated with coloured designs. From it leads a primitive wooden stair, said to be haunted by a white lady – a Billingham.

John, called the Cowherd of Billingham, married Bishop Kellaw's sister in 1248, founding a prominent local family. Thomas Billingham, when piping water from his Fram Well in Sidegate to his town house in the Market Place, granted a supply for the Market Place Pant to the Corpus Christi Guild in 1450. In 1636 Cuthbert Billingham cut the pipes to divert water to his mills at Crook Hall, but was forced to restore them. They provided the city's main supply until *c.*1850. An earlier Cuthbert Billingham, a founder, *c.* 1464, of the Silver Street maison dieu for poor travellers, accompanied Robert Lumley the hermit on pilgrimage overseas.

The Mickletons altered Crook Hall further in 1671, building a gabled extension westwards. James Mickleton, a lawyer, began to collect valuable local records known as the Mickleton-Spearman manuscripts now in the University Library.

The Hoppers of Shincliffe added the westernmost brick three-storey wing of 1736, farm buildings and the handsome granary attached to the higher of the two mills. A bird carrying a hopper or basket decorates the first-floor drawing-room ceiling, perhaps referring to their name. Their most distinguished tenant was the Reverend James Raine (1791–1858), Rector of St Mary-the-Less and Durham's indefatigable historian. His son James, the York historian, was Chancellor of York Minster; and his daughter Annie (Mrs Raine-Ellis) edited Fanny Burney's diaries, wrote a novel about late Georgian Durham clergy families, and copied designs from Cathedral Library illuminated manuscripts for Ruskin. Ruskin, like Wordsworth and Boruwlaski, visited Crook Hall. The restoration in 1983–4 of the hall and the Mickleton wing by John and Mary Hawgood, the owners until 1995, received a Civic Trust Commendation. The extensive gardens are varied and very attractive. Keith Bell, the present owner, is carrying out further restoration and has opened part of the moat which surrounded the area of the former courtyard. Visitors are admitted in the summer months during advertised opening hours (telephone: 0191 384 8028).

From Crook Hall lane, Sidegate climbs to the railway arch. Beside it stands the medieval Fram Well head, its opening sealed and with an inscribed notice of the Pant Masters, officers of St Nicholas' parish.

Field footpaths lead to a farm enclosed from the old bishops' park of Frankland, which today gives its name to a new prison.

Aykleyheads, Dryburn and North Road

The main road to Chester-le-Street and Newcastle passes through the railway arch. An unobtrusive left turning leads to Wharton Park, given to the city by W. Lloyd Wharton about 1850, with its tennis courts and spectacular views. In a garden setting on the right, the Durham Light Infantry Museum and Arts Centre offers changing exhibitions and concerts.

Left of the road junction, St Cuthbert's (Anglican) church occupies the site of the medieval St Leonard's hospital, probably where St Godric's sister died. Across the roundabout is the University Hospital of North Durham. Between them was Gibbet Knowle where Edmund Dyke, Richard Holyday, John Hogge and Richard Hill, seminary priests, were executed in 1591. Their bravery so impressed Robert Maire of Hardwick

and his young bride Grace Smith, who were present, that they became Roman Catholics. Grace, the only daughter of Henry Smith and niece of John Heath of Kepier, was disinherited by her father, who left his fortune to found Smith's charity. *(See also page 16 under Claypath for the Maire family.)* It was said that a brook near the gallows ceased to flow at the time of the execution; but the name Dryburn is older. John Boaste, another recusant priest, was executed on 24 July 1594. These priests were among the forty English martyrs canonised by Pope Paul VI on 25 October 1970.

On the right is County Hall. In its spacious entrance, where modern friezes illustrate Durham history, the County Record Office displays documents from its extensive collection which is available for research. A return to Framwellgate Bridge may be made down tree-shaded North Road. Parallel, at a higher level, is Western Hill, with the obelisk erected by W. L. Wharton in 1850 to mark the meridian 1,200 yards north of the University's observatory. North Road passes the County Hospital (opened 1853). Nearby is Waddington Street United Reformed church and, in grounds off Redhills Lane, with statues of famous miners' leaders, the impressive Miners' Hall has become the home of several educational organisations since the closure of Durham coal mines. A little way beyond, in Hawthorn Terrace, the world-famous organ factory of Harrison and Harrison flourished from 1872 but has now moved to Meadowfield. Across the North Road roundabout stands the large neo-classical North Road Methodist church near the bus station. Shops line the road to Framwellgate Bridge, dominated by the Castle.

▼ **Crook Hall: the south front** showing the Mickleton wing (right) built 1671 and left, the three-storey Hopper wing of 1736. The climbing pear trees are probably over 200 years old

▲ **Crook Hall**: the north side of the medieval hall, with replacement turret stair for access to the minstrels' gallery and upper floor of the Mickleton wing

▼ **DLI Museum and Arts Centre** tells the story of the county's regiment, the famous Durham Light Infantry, from 1758 to 1968

Crossgate or the Old Borough

Crossgate, called the Old Borough to distinguish it from the monks' new borough of Elvet created in the 12th century, was separately administered as the priors' manor. It comprised Allergate, inhabited in the 12th century, Crossgate itself (the direct road west before North Road existed) and South Street, which climbs high above the west bank of the River Wear and leads south.

St Margaret's Church

The church of St Margaret of Antioch, at the junction of Crossgate and South Street, was founded as a chapel in St Oswald's parish to serve Crossgate and Framwellgate. Increasing population necessitated the creation of separate parishes in the 19th and 20th centuries. Gracious, but heavily restored, it retains the south nave arcade and western portions of the building of *c*.1150. The chancel was extended eastwards and the north arcade built *c*.1195; the tower was rebuilt in the 14th century and the south aisle in the 15th century. Squints beside the chancel arch afford views of the high altar from north and south aisles, that to the south being cleverly contrived so that the south aisle altar is seen also from the nave. Sir John Duck (*see also page 17*) lies buried in the central aisle. An orchard in South Street and the adjacent site of the priory's fishponds became extensions to the churchyard in 1820 and 1825.

Below the church, the timber-framed end of a demolished house remains in the Fighting Cocks, a reminder of cock fighting which also took place in a cock pit in Old Elvet. Steps ascend to high footpaths in Crossgate, where 17th-century facades cloak older structures. The manorial Tolbooth was on the north side below Allergate. Crossgate continues past the former St Margaret's Hospital to a crossroads, where the Peth leads to the suburb of Neville's Cross and the cross, now a mere stump within railings opposite St John's church, commemorates the battle of 1346.

South Street, Pimlico and Durham School

From St Margaret's church, South Street climbs alongside the river. Picturesque houses face views of Cathedral and Castle, claimed to be the finest in Europe.

At the top once stood a cross, the priors' prison (abandoned in the 13th century) and their dovecote. A stone stile leads to riverside paths and Prebends' Bridge.

In nearby Pimlico is 'The Grove', once the home of Stephen Kemble, the actor who played Falstaff without padding before George IV. Opposite is the Bellasis, so-named from its 13th-century tenants and now the site of Durham School. Here (Sir) William Fothergill Cooke (1806–79), son of a Durham doctor, helped Professor Wheatstone develop the five-needle electric (railway) telegraph patented in 1837. (S. F. B. Morse is believed to have invented his electro-magnetic telegraph in 1835.)

In 1842, the Bellasis passed from the Cookes to Durham School, transferred there from Palace Green to buildings designed by Salvin (1844). The impressive chapel (1924–6) is a 1914–18 war memorial. The school's King's scholarships date from Henry VIII's new foundation following the dissolution of religious houses.

Along a leafy lane above the wooded river banks and past school playing fields a roundabout is reached. Below, the Dean and Chapter's a private road through the White Gates leads to Prebends' Bridge. Opposite is Quarry Heads Lane skirting ancient quarries beside the river; and to the right Potters Bank rises alongside the boundary between Crossgate and Elvet. Bearing left from Potters Bank are St Mary's College, St Aidan's College, the Oriental Museum and Van Mildert College.

⚊ **St Margaret of Antioch**: south side. Founded as a chapel in St Oswald's parish, it served Crossgate and Framwellgate until new parishes were formed in the 19th and 20th centuries as populations increased. The Billinghams of Crook Hall and Sir John Duck are buried here

⚊ **South Street**, once the busy centre of the Old Borough of Crossgate

Borough of Gilesgate and St Mary Magdalene

Gilesgate and St Mary Magdalene

Gilesgate may be reached from Claypath or Leazes Road. From the footbridge at the roundabout a panoramic view includes, to the west, the 1857 Victoria railway viaduct crossing North Road, County Hall, Aykleyheads, the Durham Light Infantry Museum and Crook Hall below. To the east the motorway link road follows the old railway track from the first Durham station, whose buildings overlook the roundabout. When Durham graduate Edward Bradley (as 'Cuthbert Bede') based his novel *Verdant Green* on the early university, an illustration for the first edition showed undergraduates with luggage in Gilesgate nearby. Opposite stands the ruined hospital chapel of St Mary Magdalene, consecrated in 1451 and transferred from a nearby unsatisfactory site. Its inmates, under a Master from Durham Priory's Almonry, were aged poor of the vicinity. Until the 17th century it was the church of an extra-parochial district, which was transferred to St Nicholas' parish in 1978, although the ruins remain extra-parochial. The graveyard became a garden in 1822.

College of St Hild and St Bede

Near the footbridge is the College of St Hild and St Bede, together with the University's department of education. Formerly two diocesan teacher-training colleges, St Hild's was founded in 1858 for women; and Bede College for men, begun in Framwellgate in 1841, moved here in 1846–7. Its chapel (1938–9) was designed by Seely and Paget.

Up the hill is Gilesgate Green and St Giles' church overlooking Pelaw Woods and Old Durham, where the Tempests built a new manor house which the Londonderry family inherited, but abandoned in the 18th century. Its terraced gardens overlooking the river and Maiden Castle became a mid-19th-century pleasure garden. (*For a detailed account see pages 32-34*)

St Giles' Church and Kepier Hospital

St Giles' church, founded as the chapel of Bishop Flambard's hospital of 1112, where St Godric held a minor lay office, retains its original north nave wall. During the troubles of 1144, the buildings were burnt and the present church is substantially 13th-15th-century rebuilding. In the sanctuary, an oak effigy commemorates John Heath (*d.* 1591), Warden of London's Fleet Prison, who purchased the dissolved Kepier Hospital property, including Old Durham manor. (*See also page 32*)

A footpath near St Mary Magdalene descends to Kepier Hospital to which St Giles' Hospital, for a Master and thirteen brethren, moved in about 1180. (It may be reached also from the Sands.) Contrary to popular belief, this was never a leper hospital. The brethren relieved the poor, welcomed pilgrims and entertained important visitors, including Archbishop Wickwane (1283), Edward I (1298) and Queen Isabella (1312). The surviving gateway is 14th-century and Kepier Farm is mostly 14th-century work on 12th-century foundations. Its west wall incorporates a stone crucifix and the east windows have original tracery. John, son of the first John Heath, built a mansion adjoining the southern medieval buildings. The remaining loggia is the only one of its period in the county.

⌂ **Kepier Hospital gateway**: the inner side. The barns to the right, later enclosed in stone and brick, are timber-framed. They had new roof timbers about 1450

✎ **College of St Hild and St Bede**

▽ **St Giles' church**, founded in 1112 as the chapel of Bishop Flambard's Hospital, which moved to Kepier by the river

Elvet

Elvet is probably Aelfet-ee 'swan island' where in 762, Peohtwine was consecrated Bishop of Whithorn in Galloway, once part of Northumbria.

In monastic times, Elvet was administered by Durham Priory's hostillar, who held manorial courts here, and was responsible for the furnishing and fabric of the parish church. The extensive parish then included all of the land outside the loop of the river, with the chapelries of St Margaret's, Witton Gilbert, and Croxdale (now separate parishes), in addition to Finchale Priory, where the present congregation of St Oswald's still holds an annual Ascension Day evening Communion service in the ruined church.

The ancient parish was probably a large Anglo-Saxon estate.

St Oswald's Church

The dedication is to St Oswald, who became a Christian during his exile with his brother and sister on Iona, in the monastery founded by Columba. Later, as King of Northumbria, reigning from Bamburgh, Oswald invited St Aidan from Iona to settle on Lindisfarne (Holy Island) and to found there a monastery from which to send missionaries to convert his extensive kingdom to the Christian faith. Many early dedications to St Oswald reflect the work of St Aidan and his immediate successors. King Oswald died in 642 fighting Penda, pagan King of Mercia, at Maserfield near Oswestry. His severed head was later placed in St Cuthbert's coffin, now in Durham Cathedral.

The church's chancel arch and the four eastern bays of the nave, with rounded-headed arches and round columns, are of c. 1195, and survive a 14th-century rebuilding of both chancel and north aisle. The fine chancel stalls are early 15th-century woodwork; and clerestory and tower are also 15th-century work. Subsidence, once thought to be due to Elvet Colliery working, but caused by walls built over earlier burials, led to

the restorations of 1834, 1864 and 1883. (Although coal seams lie below the church, they are too thin to work.) The chancel and south aisle walls, which had recesses for recumbent effigies, were rebuilt. A fine pre-Reformation roof with painted panels was also lost. Its wooden corbels were carved into grotesque heads which still look down into the nave.

In 1864 a delicately hued west window by Ford Madox Brown (associate of William Morris) was inserted in the tower. It depicts the life of St Oswald from the time of his baptism on Iona.

The tower stairs, a straight flight rising in the thickness of its south wall, use twenty-four reversed 13th-14th-century grave covers. Their carved designs may be seen overhead on ascending the steps to the belfry. Some incorporate swords (gentry) or occupational symbols: e.g. a horn on a cord (a forester), a mattock (a husbandman), a hatchet (a woodcutter).

Anglo-Saxon sculptured stones, parts of crosses used later as building blocks by medieval builders, were found in the tower's west wall and in the churchyard wall bordering Church Street, suggesting a pre-Conquest church here before the Community of St Cuthbert settled on the Durham Peninsula. These sculptures are displayed in the dormitory of Durham Cathedral.

The vicar from 1862 to 1874 was John Bacchus Dykes, the hymn writer. He named his familiar tune to *Jesu, lover of my soul*, 'Hollingside'. He lived at Hollingside cottage, near Hollingside Wood in the parish, near the University's Botanic Garden. He is buried in the graveyard opposite the church.

Two wall tablets are of special interest. At the east end of the south aisle, an oval memorial commemorates George Smith of Burn Hall, son of the Reverend John Smith, Canon of Durham and editor of a scholarly edition of the Venerable Bede's *Historic Works*. George Smith, who bought Burn Hall (in the parish) in 1717, was a Non-juror (one who refused the Oath of Allegiance to William and Mary) who took holy orders in the Non-juring church and became its titular Bishop of Durham. He died in 1756. The other notable wall tablet is the exceptionally fine Elizabethan memorial (*see page 45*) at the east end of the north aisle, commemorating Christopher Chaytor of Butterby, in the chapelry of Croxdale, who died in 1592, aged 98.

▶ **St Oswald's church**: one of a series of grotesque corbels supporting the nave roof

◀ **St Oswald's church**, the south side. Its western tower stands close to the riverside footpath from the ancient churchyard to Prebends' Bridge

◢ **St Oswald's church**: the west gallery of 1987

▶ **St Oswald's church**: the west window by William Morris & Co tells the story of St Oswald and his relics: baptism, coronation, sending missionaries into Northumbria, Cadwallon's death, the slaying of King Oswald, his body enshrined. The coats of arms are in memory of John Fogg-Elliot of Elvet Hill, *d.* 1881

◣ **St Oswald's church**: medieval cross of latten (an alloy of copper and zinc) with figures of Mary and the apostle John beside the crucifix

A dowsing survey, carried out in 1982, showed the plan of an earlier church. It had an eastern apse and a shorter nave flanked by north and south porticuses (side-chambers of Anglo-Saxon type). At the west end, within the present nave's fifth bay, a square structure may have been a tower or narthex. At this point the round pillars of the later nave continue with octagonal ones, making two further bays. Evidence of the medieval rood loft stair may be traced in the eastern pillar of the south aisle. The chancel stalls are early 15th-century. A fine medieval cross of latten, with figures of Mary and the apostle John beside a crucifix, and designed either to stand on an altar or be mounted as a processional cross, was given to J.B. Dykes after it was found in a mail coach in Elvet. It is used now to lead processions on special occasions.

In July 1983, the installation of a new heating system provided an opportunity for limited archaeological excavations to check the dowsing survey at the east end of the north aisle. A north-south trench revealed a feature pre-dating the present north wall of *c.* 1350, probably a pre-Norman outer north wall within it.

A fire which started in the chancel's organ bay on 7 March (Ash Wednesday) 1984 did extensive damage and destroyed the organ. The new organ, which was completed in 1988, was planned by Nicholas Thistlethwaite, designed by Henry Moss and built by Peter Collins. It occupies a new west gallery (1987) reviving a traditional post-Reformation site before the 19th-century introduction of robed choirs in chancels.

Below are raked semi-circular choir stalls. The organ, of original design, has the now favoured and revived simple mechanical action, and three keyboards, with the great organ and pedal organ in the main case, the swell organ behind it, and the choir organ in a small case at the front of the gallery. The pipes of hammered lead have a mellowed appearance; the carving by Siegfried Pietszch was inspired by notable early 17th-century examples stylistically consistent with Bishop John Cosin's work at Durham Cathedral, Brancepeth and Auckland Castle, and with bracket motifs from Gabriel Krammer's pattern book circulated in 1610. The gallery, designed to relate to the new north door screen, inspired by box pews at Ninekirk (1661), has a balustrade reminiscent of work at Rycote chapel, Oxfordshire, c. 1630. Concerts frequently take place here, continuing the church's fine musical tradition.

Adjacent to the wall south of the churchyard was a hermit's cell or anchorage; and the tomb of St John Wharton, an anchorite, became a pilgrim shrine in the church before the Reformation.

On the steep bank below the tower is St Oswald's Well, a clear spring, which once had an elegant arcaded well-head and platform, destroyed by vandals.

A footpath leaves Church Street by the war memorial cross, passing between the tower and St Oswald's Well to a tree-shaded walk high above the river to Prebends' Bridge.

Church Street and South Road

Church Street leads past Anchorage Terrace, built in connection with George and Henry Salvin's new cotton factory. They brought machinery here from Castle Eden in 1796, when a river and canal scheme to establish Durham as an industrial centre was revived. The factory burnt down in 1804 and was never rebuilt. When Elvet pit was sunk, the houses became 'Pit Row', but after the pit's late 19th-century closure were renamed Anchorage Terrace from the nearby site of the anchorage.

At the crossroads, Quarry Heads Lane turns right by a playing field opposite the New Inn. In the hedge stands the stump of Charley's Cross (formerly Peaseby's Cross) which was moved from the opposite side of the crossroads. It was once a boundary or sanctuary cross.

Opposite is South Road. On the left corner are the University's science laboratories and the new University Library (1982). Beyond on the left are Grey College (1959) and Collingwood College (1971). On the right is Trevelyan College (1967) and a lane to Van Mildert College (1965) and St Aidan's College (1964), near Elvet Hill House, former home of the architect Ignatius Bonomi, and now the University's Oriental Department. The magnificent Museum of Oriental Art, added in 1959, is open to the public (*see page 31*).

Hallgarth Street

Returning to the crossroads, the road east joins Hallgarth Street at Mount Joy, overlooked by high ground. Tradition claims that the Community of St Cuthbert first saw the Durham Peninsula from here when they arrived in 995 with the body of St Cuthbert, to settle and build their great church. The road to the south (A177) leads through tree-shaded Shincliffe Peth past Houghall Agricultural College. Behind houses on the east side of Hallgarth Street stood the hostillar's hall or home farm. The fine half-timbered tithe barn and checker of 1446–7 are now a prison officers' club. The substantial stone building at right angles to the street is also medieval and was part of the farm complex. Opposite stands Hallgarth House, of five bays, built about 1700 of brick with stone dressing and stone bands

Hallgarth Street: the checker of 1446–7, over a wagon shed, where Durham Priory's officer conducted business relating to tithes on crops in Elvet

above the windows; an extension of four bays, now a separate house, matches the original. Behind is a large garden with mature trees.

New Elvet

Hallgarth Street leads down to New Elvet. Beyond the junction with Church Street, Kingsgate Bridge on the left crosses the river as pedestrian access to the peninsula. Beside it Dunelm House (student centre), and Elvet Riverside (University arts lecture rooms) are opposite Court Lane which follows the boundary between Elvet barony and the monks' borough of Elvet.

Below Court Lane, the large double-fronted 18th-century house is now the Durham City Police Headquarters. It was owned in the early 19th century by John Gregson, an attorney. During the 1930s, when the top front windows retained nursery safety bars, the ghost of a small girl, in a long skirt, cap and button boots, with her hands in a muff, sometimes appeared in a top landing doorway singing nursery rhymes. She has been associated with the name Anne Gregson scratched with a diamond above the date 1808 in a south-end rear window. She has re-appeared more recently.

Court Lane leads to the head of Old Elvet and New Elvet joins the foot of Old Elvet at Elvet Bridge.

Old Elvet

Facing pleasant gardens at the head of Old Elvet stand the combined Assize Courts, by Francis Sandys (1809–11) and Durham Prison, completed in 1819 by Moneypenny and Ignatius Bonomi. St Cuthbert's church opposite, also by Bonomi (1827), symbolises Old Elvet's reputation as a refuge for Roman Catholics under persecution. Old Elvet was a 15th-century road south.

Its broad street, graced by dignified Georgian façades, accommodated horse fairs until early in the 20th century. Outside no. 21, next to the Courts, one lamp standard remains of several erected in 1824 to contend with disorder in unlit streets. They burnt whale oil from Hull. The elegant balcony of no. 30 overlooks the site of Old Elvet's public well among trees. Lady Elizabeth Milbanke, relative of Byron's wife, once lived at no. 34, as later did the Reverend J. B. Dykes. The Masonic Hall, a mock-gothic design by T.C. Ebdy (1869), the Old Shire Hall (1895–7), now University offices, and Elvet Methodist church with its spire (1903) break a former stylistic unity.

The Royal County Hotel was formerly two houses. The handsome staircase of 1680, from the demolished Stroughton Hall, near Leicester, was installed in the hotel in 1926. Lady Mary Radclyffe (a member of the Derwentwater family of Dilston) had occupied one house, maintaining there 'Mr Ferdinando Ashmole, a Popish priest' whose burial was recorded at St Oswald's.

Her half-sister was Lady Mary Tudor, natural daughter of Charles II; James, her nephew, was executed after the 1715 rebellion; and his brother Charles allegedly hid there before his arrest for treason after the 1745 rebellion. Elizabeth Bowes, aunt of Lord Strathmore's wife, Mary Eleanor Bowes, owned the house from 1758. On the hotel balcony, between 18th-century pilasters, leading politicians appear on the third Saturday of July each year at the Durham Miners' Gala. Members of miners' lodges follow their banners and bands to the playing-fields (Smiddyhaughs – 'smooth river meadows'), which were Durham's Race Course from 1733–1887. Since the closing of the Durham pits, the Miners' Gala has lost much of its impetus and its future is uncertain. (*See also picture on page 13.*)

Through the archway was Chapel Passage, now demolished, named from a Wesleyan chapel opened there in 1808. (John Wesley, who died in 1791, probably preached in an earlier chapel, a converted house in Court Lane which has also vanished.) Beyond is the elegant former Masonic Hall, begun in 1809. At the corner, the Waterloo, a former coaching inn, was destroyed in 1971 to give access to the new bridge.

Elvet Bridge (Elvet end)

From here, pedestrians should use the medieval bridge to reach the city centre. At the Elvet end of the bridge on the left, on a bridge pillar beside a formerly 'wet' arch, the remains of St Andrew's chapel, founded between 1274 and 1284 by William son of Absolam, are camouflaged by a Dutch-gabled building. After the dissolution of the chantries it had various uses. In the 18th century it was used partly as a blacksmith's shop (and remained so until the early 19th century); while a charity school was taught in what appeared to have been the chancel. (*See also page 13.*)

Elvet Bridge rising towards the site of the former bridge tower

The Banks

Steps lead from the foot of Silver Street to the riverside. The upper footpath mounts beside the crenellated wall of the Castle's Fellows' garden, formerly the private garden of the bishops, built west of the earlier fortifications. From this path, Windy Gap (site of the medieval Windishole Postern) branches up to Palace Green. The path leads past the former Broken Walls quarry, which caused the collapse of Bishop Flambard's fortification wall. From here in 1663 stone was quarried for Castle restoration. The path continues below the Cathedral's west end to join the lower one near Prebends' Bridge. Between the upper and lower paths is St Cuthbert's Well, its well-head dated 1690, which was restored in 1987. It was provided after the Galilee Well's outer dip-well (*see page 7*), now visible only below a grating in the subsequently raised path, could no longer be used by the public.

Water was obtained from several springs in the Banks and wells sunk near to the Cathedral and Castle. In this region ground water collects in permeable sandstone near to the surface which overlies a thin coal seam and a layer of impermeable clay. Springs occur where the water escapes above the clay bands in the sides of the Banks, such as at St Cuthbert's Well and St Oswald's Well (*see page 23*). Wells sunk through the sandstone bands to the clay beneath provide a good water supply, like those in the College and some of the houses in the Bailey.

On the lower footpath, the two former corn mills were known from *c*.1500 as the Jesus Mills, as their profits financed the Cathedral's Jesus (nave) altar. The buildings now form the Old Fulling Mill, the University's Museum of Archaeology (*see also page 31*). One mill was leased in 1792 for carding and fulling, a process of cleaning cloth using fuller's earth.

The weir served also two mills opposite for corn and fulling. The river is popular for boating, and Durham School and individual colleges own boathouses.

Prebends' Bridge, designed by George Nicholson (1777), replaced a wooden footbridge of 1574 and a stone bridge of 1696, swept away except for abutments up-river, in the 1771 flood. The monks had a ferry here to Crossgate Manor. A plaque is inscribed with a verse by Sir Walter Scott:

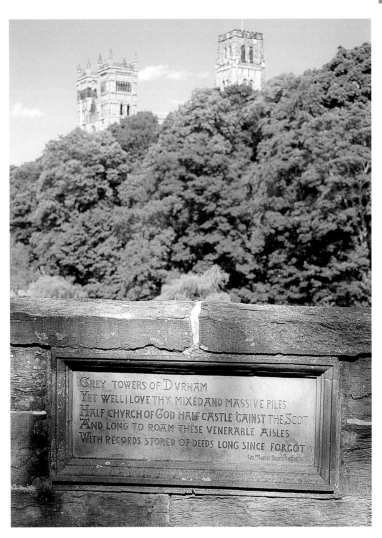

▲ **Prebends' Bridge**, with verse by Sir Walter Scott

Grey towers of Durham –
Yet well I love thy mixed and massive piles,
Half church of God, half castle 'gainst the Scot –
And long to roam those venerable aisles
With records stored of deeds long since forgot.

Colin Wilbourn of Sunderland carved the Kathedra, a large stone sculpture beneath Prebends' Bridge. Its name recalls that the word Cathedral is derived from the Latin *cathedra*, the seat from which a bishop in early times taught his followers. The sculptor was Artist-in-Residence in Durham Cathedral in 1986–7 and the first local person to hold this annual appointment, living in St Chad's College and financed by the Dean and Chapter of Durham Cathedral and Northern Arts. Another sculpture from the same hand may be seen in the University Botanic Garden (*see page 31*).

On the west bank two rising paths lead, right, to South Street (one passes South Street well, a strong clear spring); the road is to the White Gates and Quarry Heads Lane, named from the monastic sacrists' quarry which supplied stone for the Cathedral. The left path follows the river to St Oswald's churchyard, or, by branching right beside a cascading stream, climbs to Church Street head. Bases of turrets among the trees mark former air shafts to Elvet Colliery whose pit-head is now the University science site.

Returning across Prebends' Bridge, the road leads to South Bailey. The footpath, right, continues beside the river past the misnamed 'Counts' House' (c. 1820–30), a classical-style garden house which belonged to 12, South Bailey. (See also page 15 for 'Count' Boruwlaski.) Below, nearer the river, once stood the cottage where the Misses Ebdon kept house for the 'Little Count'.

Nearby is the long course finishing post of England's oldest regatta, established in 1834, some years before Henley. The path continues, with the Peninsula walls high above, to pass beneath Kingsgate Bridge. Fearon's Path, connecting Bow Lane steps and Elvet Bridge, was paved by Dr Andrewes Fearon of Winchester, Durham School's headmaster 1882–4, to benefit both town and University rowing enthusiasts.

Boats may be hired at Brown's boathouse, between Elvet Bridge and New Elvet Bridge, and paths follow the river past Baths Bridge, named from the nearby swimming baths, to continue in pleasant riverside walks.

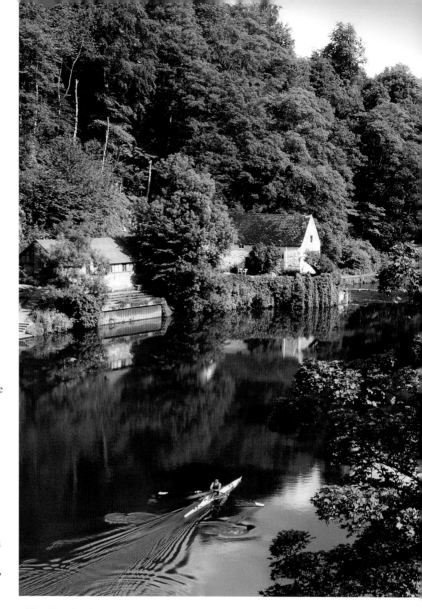

▲ **River Wear** from Prebends' Bridge, with boathouse and old corn mill

▼ **The misnamed 'Count's House': a folly**, formerly a gardener's cottage attached to 12, South Bailey

▼ **Josef Boruwlaski**, the so-called 'Little Count', from the portrait in the Town Hall

University of Durham

History

Durham, the fourth oldest English University, began as a purely ecclesiastical foundation on 28 October 1833. It originated in the Cathedral Chapter Act of 1831, which led to the Durham University Bill of 1832. Under Archdeacon Thorp as Warden, 19 foundation scholars and 18 others took up residence in Archdeacon's Inn, Palace Green. A Royal Charter was granted in 1837.

The bishops' castle, granted with church estates in 1839–40, provided the new University College with a hall larger and more beautiful than any at Oxford and incomparable buildings.

There had been earlier university schemes. From *c.* 1286 Durham Priory sent promising young monks to Durham Hall, Oxford, which became an endowed College in 1380. As monastic property, Durham College surrendered to Henry VIII, who planned to re-found it with a provost, 4 readers, 9 scholars, 10 divinity students at Oxford and 10 at Cambridge, a schoolmaster and an usher (assistant master). Durham's new Dean and Chapter returned it to the King in 1544 and it passed in 1556 to Trinity College (founded 1555) with Durham connections severed.

After the Castle and Cathedral passed into secular hands under the Commonwealth, Parliament received three general local petitions (1649–52) inspired, perhaps, by an unsuccessful Elizabethan plan for a college at Ripon to serve the North. Following a fourth petition, presented personally to Oliver Cromwell in 1657, the mayor and aldermen were instructed to 'set out so much of the Cathedral as shall be necessary for a chapel and schooles'. The College was to be financed by sequestered Cathedral funds and subscriptions. Letters Patent of 14 May 1657 provided for a provost, 2 preachers or senior fellows, 12 fellows (i.e. 4 professors, 4 tutors and 4 schoolmasters – in the Oxford sense), with endowments for 24 scholars and 12 exhibitioners; while the 'free school' was attached under existing masters. University status, petitioned for immediately, was opposed successfully by Oxford and Cambridge. Cromwell died in 1658; and when the monarchy was restored in 1660, the Cathedral and its revenues reverted to the re-constituted Dean and Chapter. The infant college closed.

The scheme of 1831 succeeded and the University, like its predecessors at Oxford and Cambridge, is collegiate. Its colleges and other buildings are scattered widely throughout the city and its outskirts.

In 1839, the University purchased astronomical instruments and a telescope. The architect Anthony Salvin designed an **Observatory** which was built by public subscription in 1841 south-west of the Peninsula; and the Duke of Northumberland presented a refractory telescope in 1846. It was removed when the building was refurbished in the 1960s. An obelisk erected on Western Hill by W. L. Wharton in 1850 marks the meridian

Hatfield College

1,200 yards north. The Observatory holds the longest weather records in England, kept since 1847 (now in the University Library), for which it has been commended recently by the Meteorological Office.

Hatfield College, named after Bishop Thomas Hatfield (1345–81), was founded in 1846 in the old Red Lion coaching inn and elegant assembly rooms of *c.* 1770 (*see page 12*) which remain, with the chapel of 1853, the nucleus of its present college buildings in the North Bailey. It is, therefore, one of the oldest provincial establishments in the country and at present accommodates undergraduate and post-graduate students, whose studies cover the entire spectrum of courses in the University.

Following the success of Hatfield, Archdeacon's Inn on Palace Green was revived in 1851 as Bishop Cosin's Hall, but had to be closed in 1864. It now serves as an additional accommodation for University College.

Growth was slow, but Newcastle upon Tyne's **Durham College of Medicine** (1870) and **Durham**

▲ **St Cuthbert's Society**: the main building, 12, South Bailey, with its adjacent properties
◀ **St Cuthbert's Society**: 18th-century door head, matching another in North Bailey once belonging to the same owner, i.e. residence and solicitors' offices

College of Science (1871) greatly increased student intake. The affiliated Codrington College, Barbados, and Fourah Bay College, Sierra Leone, also granted Durham degrees.

Intending teachers were admitted to **Bede College** for men (1841) with buildings 1845–7 and **St Hild's College** for women (1858), both Church of England Diocesan Training Colleges. These united as the College of St Hild and St Bede, which became a member college of the University in 1979.

Unattached or non-collegiate students were first admitted to the University in 1871; and as numbers increased, they developed a corporate life for social and athletic activities. **St Cuthbert's Society**, founded in 1888, has been based in South Bailey since 1951. It became a mixed society in 1969. Eighty of its 400 members – about a third of whom are mature students – live in South Bailey and the rest in other city properties.

Women were first admitted to degrees by a supplemental charter of 1895, obtained through the energy of Dean Waddington. Four St Hild's students enrolled immediately and 'Home' students followed.

A women's hostel opened in 1899 in Abbey House, Palace Green and became **St Mary's College** in 1919. It transferred to Elvet Hill in 1952. **St Chad's** Hall, in North Bailey, and **St John's** Hall in South Bailey, were founded in 1904 and 1909 mainly, but not solely, for Anglican candidates for the ministry; and both are now Colleges. St John's added subsequently Cranmer Hall for their post-graduate training, to which women were admitted in 1966. St John's became open to women undergraduates from 1973 and St Chad's from 1988 (*see also text on page 12*).

Essential local expansion off the Peninsula began in 1924 with the Dawson Building, South Road, containing the first botany, chemistry, geology and physics laboratories. The west buildings were added in 1950–1 with the Appleby Theatre, designed by

Clockwise, from above: **St Mary's College**: main building; **St Chad's College**; **Grey College**; **St Aidan's College**; **St John's College**

J. S. Allen. Expansion on the Science Site has continued to the present day.

Grey College, founded in 1959, occupies the adjacent Fountains Field, from whose natural springs Durham Priory obtained water piped across the river. The College is named after the 2nd Earl Grey who, as Prime Minister, signed the Bill founding Durham University. Its quadrangles and detached buildings are arranged to command the widest possible views of the city. The doors to its dining hall were presented and were once a part of the annexe to Westminster Abbey built for the coronation of Queen Elizabeth II.

A second body of women 'Home' students, using a variety of houses, became **St Aidan's** Society in 1947 and a College in 1961. In 1964 it moved to new buildings on the hill above St Mary's College and close to the Oriental Department and Museum. It now has both men and women members.

The Graduate Society, which was formed in 1965 for post-graduate students, was re-named **Ustinov College** in April 2003 after Sir Peter Ustinov, the University's Chancellor from 1992, who was present for the official re-naming at Howlands Farm (off South Road) where

▲ **Van Mildert College**
◄ **Collingwood College**
▼ **Trevelyan College**

expansion is planned. The College claims to be the largest college for post-graduates in the country with over 1,250 members. Sir Peter died on 29 March 2004.

Van Mildert College, opened in 1966, is named after Bishop William Van Mildert, last of the prince-bishops and a founder of the University. Its pleasant site off South Road is enhanced by a lake with fish and wild fowl.

Trevelyan College followed in 1967 on the opposite corner of Mill Hill Lane in tranquil wooded surroundings. The unusual architecture was designed by John Eastwick-Field. Its name commemorates George Macaulay Trevelyan (of Wallington Hall, Northumberland), Regius Professor of Modern History at Cambridge University 1927–40, Master of Trinity College, Cambridge 1940–51 and Chancellor of Durham University 1950–58.

Collingwood College, founded in 1971, is named after Sir Edward Collingwood, Chairman of the University Council 1963–70. It has the distinction of being the first to be founded as a mixed college. The first students entered in 1972. The monumental buildings, dominated internally by restful vistas of surrounding trees, lie near the site of Oswald House, whose wooded grounds have been used by the architect, Richard Sheppard of London, as an integral part of his scheme.

Kingsgate Bridge, designed by Ove Arup, was built jointly by the University and the city to connect the peninsula with the new developments in Elvet to the east and south-east, where the latest building is the main **University Library**, begun in 1982 at the corner of South Road (*see also pages 5 and 23*). **Dunelm House**, at the eastern end of the footbridge, contains the Student and Staff Centre, which has facilities for visitors during vacations.

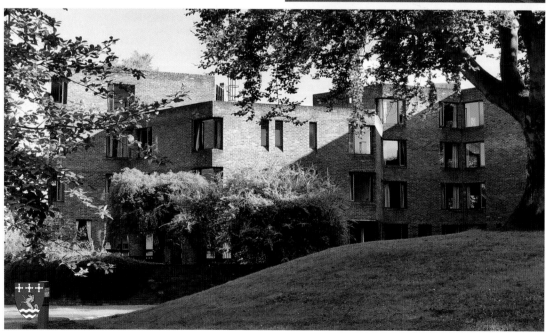

Museum of Archaeology

The Museum of Archaeology occupies the Old Fulling Mill (formerly two corn mills) below the Cathedral's western towers and welcomes visitors (*see also page 25*). The Department of Archaeology has conducted numerous excavations on Roman and medieval sites, including those in the city and some of the discoveries are displayed here attractively.

Among them is material from the ruined medieval manor house of the Prior of Durham at Bearpark (Beaurepaire), 2–3 miles west of the city. The site, which belongs to the City Council, is open to the public and has a picnic area (*see pages 38–39*).

Temporary displays are held in the refurbished upper gallery.

Oriental Museum

One of the less obvious treasures of Durham, the collection of Oriental Art, is housed in the Durham University Oriental Museum. It consists primarily of three major divisions, the Chinese ceramics collected by the Right Honourable Malcolm MacDonald who was Chancellor of the University from 1970 to 1981; the collection of Egyptian antiquities made by the 4th Duke of Northumberland in the 1820s; and a vast group of Chinese jade and other hardstone carvings given to the University by Sir Charles Hardinge. These are supplemented by objects from other parts of the Orient and the result is regarded by connoisseurs all over the world as a major museum of oriental art.

Botanic Garden

The University of Durham Botanic Garden covers 18 acres in the woodland and countryside 1 mile south of Durham city. Mature trees shelter some of the more unusual plants collected from all over the world. Two small glass houses, one for rainforest plants and the other for cacti, are popular with visitors. There is a waterfall and a pool stocked with fish.

The new Alpine Garden is made up of two raised beds and a limestone Rock Garden. The south aspect creates a micro-climate which also provides a sheltered place for visitors to sit.

The Woodland and Primula Gardens are best seen in

Botanic Garden: pool and two of the three fountains

spring, while the rose pergola is a summer feature. Heathers and rich autumn colours on the North American trees are spectacular at other times. The award-winning Prince Bishop's Garden, designed and sponsored by Durham County Council for the Gateshead Garden Festival, was relocated at the Botanic Garden in the summer of 1991. The theme of the figures by Colin Wilbourn is 'In the shadow of the past'. Treated trunks of trees, which had died of Dutch elm disease, were used from Houghall Agricultural College, Durham, and from Wolsingham, Weardale. Each figure is shadowed by steel fretwork which, if viewed from a central area, becomes a relevant scene. The first group represents William of St Calais (Carilef), bishop 1081–96, responsible for Durham Cathedral's chancel and choir aisles; the shadow shows the Cathedral today. Ralph, Lord Neville of Raby (*d.* 1367), commander at the victory of Neville's Cross in 1346: the shadow is Raby Castle; and John Cosin, bishop 1660–72, restorer after the Civil War and Commonwealth: the shadow depicts his chapel at Auckland Castle. The second group relates to the industrial era: a member of the Shafto family, leading county colliery owners: the shadow illustrates the pit-head and winding gear at Seaham; George Stephenson, 1781–1848, pioneer of railways: his shadow is the railway viaduct, Chester-le-Street and thirdly Sir James Laing, *b.* 1823, representing shipbuilding on the Wear, shadowed by Sunderland shipyards.

◄ ◄ **The Lafcadio Hearn Cultural Centre**: Teikyo University of Japan in Durham, Mill Hill Lane

◄ **Oriental Museum**

Places to visit in the neighbourhood

Old Durham and Old Durham Gardens

Old Durham, 1 mile east of the city, is reached either by a riverside path (15 minutes' walk), or by a lane leading south from Sherburn Road. River trips are planned to Strawberry Landing beside the wildflower meadow below the gardens. (For Maiden Castle, Roman and Dark Age remains *see* inside front cover.)

Early History

A road formerly ran from the south through Old Durham, crossing higher ground to the north before dropping to a ford at Kepier. In 1782 John Cade, the antiquary, conjectured it was Roman. The name Old Durham occurs in the earliest local documents, suggesting an ancient settlement.

By the 12th century William, rector of St Nicholas, held the manor of Old Durham where a later rector, Galfrid de Helme, obtained permission for an oratory in his 'court' in 1268. Rectors held manorial courts at Old Durham for their tenants. Their house possibly suffered before 1330 when the Scots burnt Sherburn Hospital.

The River Wear changed its course forming, in the 15th century, a partly dried-up ox-bow lake north of Maiden Castle. Both old and new river beds appear on a plan made *c.* 1440–50 when questions arose about Durham Priory's liability to maintain a road tending to flood near Scaltok Mill at Old Durham.

In 1443, Bishop Robert Neville granted the rectory of St Nicholas to Kepier Hospital, which afterwards appointed a stipendiary curate to the church, while the income from Old Durham manor augmented the revenues of the hospital (*see page 20*).

In 1474, Robert Booth, Master of Kepier, leased the manor to his brother, Richard, for 99 years (reserving the timber of Pelaw Wood and £10 rent).

When religious houses were dissolved in 1546, the Crown confiscated Kepier Hospital property. After passing through several hands, John Heath, a wealthy Protestant merchant, Warden of the Fleet Prison in London (and sometime of Kings Lynn), acquired it in 1569. He resided in the old hospital, and was probably the only purchaser of former northern religious property to do so. Noted for his generosity, he doubled the endowment of Kepier Grammar School at Houghton-le-Spring, and was granted arms (*'party per chevron, or and sable, in chief two mullets, in base a heathcock, counterchanged'*).

His purchase was subject to the lease of Old Durham. When a later Robert Booth died in 1592, he left by will the house and other property to his wife and children under age. The inventory lists a hall, many chambers, including a chapel chamber and chambers in the curtain wall, and seems typical of medieval courtyard houses, with, in its courtyard, stabling and men-at-arms' quarters above. Robert had recently bought a house in Old Elvet.

John Heath died in 1591. An oak recumbent effigy in St Giles' chancel represents him in Elizabethan plate armour, with his head resting on a tilting helmet with the Heath cock crest.

His son John Heath II succeeded him, built Kepier House and died there in 1618. As heir he left his eldest son John III, then 49, the last at Kepier, whose only child Thomas died in infancy in 1594.

The title to the Kepier property was vested in Thomas Heath of Kepier West Grange whose son, John Heath IV (1604–65) when barely 19, married Margaret, daughter of William Smith of Durham, in 1623. In December 1630, Thomas and John IV sold the house, gardens and orchards of Kepier to Ralph Cole of Gateshead, whose son and grandson resided there until 1674, although John Heath III lived there until his death in January 1640.

Old Durham Gardens: gazebo, steps and terrace

The Heaths and Tempests

Old Durham was settled on John IV and Margaret in 1630, but they lived in North Bailey. Their only child Elizabeth was baptised in October 1626 at St Mary-le-Bow, where John IV was churchwarden and in 1637 gave the strip of land on its north side for its churchyard. In February 1642 he was still a parishioner, described as 'Counsellor at lawe', and on 27 October that year Elizabeth married there John Tempest of the Isle (near Sedgefield), son of Sir Thomas Tempest, Attorney-General of Ireland.

John Heath IV was living at Old Durham in 1652, and died there in 1665, when John Tempest and Elizabeth succeeded him.

John Tempest I of Old Durham, described in a political pamphlet of 1677 as 'a papist, a pensioner, and a court-dinner man', became a strong supporter of the exiled James II. His eldest daughter, Margaret, married Sir Richard Shuttleworth of Forcett (south of Gainford) and when Elizabeth died in October 1684 and John I in July 1697 (both buried at Forcett), William, their eldest surviving son, inherited Old Durham. William had married in 1677 (at Forcett), Elizabeth, daughter of John Sudbury, Dean of Durham, and was MP for Durham city in 1678, 1680 and 1689. In 1699 he was known as Colonel Tempest; he died in March 1700 and was buried at St Giles.

His son and heir, John Tempest II (1679–1737), became MP for the county in 1705 and in the following year married the heiress Jane Wharton; but by 1719 they had left Old Durham for Sherburn while John's mother, Elizabeth, lived in Old Elvet where she died in June 1728. John died in 1737, a few months after his wife, and their son John Tempest III (1710–76) inherited the estates. He married Frances Shuttleworth of Forcett, at Merrington, in May 1738 and was MP for the city of Durham 1741–61. He bought Wynyard in 1742 but was living at Sherburn when he made his will in 1771. At Old Durham he employed a gardener, James, to maintain the gardens. John Tempest III was buried at St Giles on 17 May 1776.

His son and heir, John Tempest IV, of Wynyard (and Brancepeth Castle) married Anne Townshend, and was MP for Durham between 1768 and 1790. An estate plan drawn up for him in September 1776 shows there were two upper walled gardens, with a path alongside their joint long western wall, the gardens below this sloping towards the Beck, a formal garden with geometrically laid-out walks north of the mansion site adjacent to Pelaw Woods, and a bridle road leading from Durham across a ford and skirting the western side of the gardens to join the present lane at Old Durham Farm.

An account of the 1780s describes the gardens:

Old Durham house is gone to decay, nothing now remaining but apartments for a farmer...The gardens are formed into terraces of considerable length. This sweet retirement is become a place for public resort, where concerts of sweet music have been frequently performed in the summer, and the company regaled with fruit, tea, etc. The gardens are open all summer for rural recreation. At the corner of the garden some few years ago were the remains of a very ancient building, with a circular window, and other appearances of the chapel form.

Excavations here in the 1960s revealed stone walls with medieval hard plaster on the interior surface.

The only child of John Tempest IV was John Wharton Tempest who died unmarried aged 21 at Brighton in 1793. John IV died in 1794, and was buried at St Giles. The entire inheritance now passed to descendants of his sister Frances, who had married, at St Mary-le-Bow in 1768, the Reverend Sir Henry Vane, LL.D. (1729–94), Rector of Long Newton and a Canon of Durham Cathedral.

Their son Sir Henry Vane (1771–1813) assumed the additional name of Tempest on inheriting the Tempest estates in accordance with his uncle's will.

The 19th Century

A plan of 1812 shows Old Durham divided into farms. Other details are omitted, but the gardens and adjoining house were let to 'Jos. Robinson'. Sir Henry Vane-Tempest's wife was Anne, Countess of Antrim, and their daughter Frances Anne Emily Vane-Tempest (1800–65) married Charles William Stewart (1778–1854), 3rd Marquess of Londonderry (*see page 14*).

By 1827 the Pineapple Inn stood on part of the site and remained a public house until the licence was lost in 1926 owing to its unfavourable reputation. The historian, Robert Surtees, who died in 1834 wrote:

The house of Old Durham, the deserted seat of the Heaths and Tempests, stands warm and sheltered... The main body of the house has been taken down; the gardens only remain formed into sloping banks and long terraces. An old summerhouse, with a small bay-window, has the initials J[ohn] H[eath].

In 1849 the Londonderrys sank the Lord Ernest Pit to the Hutton seam and production continued until the end of the 19th century.

The first OS map of 1857 shows the north formal garden replanted as an orchard; the south walled garden was a bowling green, with the gazebo (its first firm appearance on a plan or map) at the west end of a raised terrace.

A 1924 *Guide to Durham* advertises Old Durham Gardens: 'Dancing, putting green, running track, tennis courts, ices, tea gardens and full licensed free house. Parties catered for'. A photograph taken from the back of the Pineapple shows four statues, one in a central flower bed. Older residents remember the running track below the slope of the lower garden with a small building for equipment against the stone wall at the north end.

Recent History

In 1893 the North Eastern Railway Company opened a station at Elvet. Branching off the line at Sherburn, this line crossed the Old Durham Estate and ran across the south-west corner of the lower garden on an embankment (still remaining). At the end of its life in the mid-1950s, it was used solely for carrying passengers to and from the annual Miners' Gala.

In 1918 the 7th Marquess of Londonderry sold the Old Durham Estate in three lots chiefly to their former tenants, the Hopps family, who still farm most of it today.

Part of the gardens was sold to St Hild's College in the 1930s for a proposed extension, never achieved, and then to the City Council in 1985 when Richard Hopps sold the adjacent land to enable restoration.

Archaeological work has revealed a series of flights of steps *c.* 9 ft wide descending from the gazebo. The wall to its north is ancient; at its north end (in a private garden) are the remains of what may have been a garderobe, and blocked mullioned windows occur in various places in neighbouring walls, all on private property. Built into the wall to the east of the Pineapple is a door pediment and much weathered coat of arms. The adjacent farm buildings are 17th–18th-century.

Pittington

The Community of St Cuthbert owned the ancient settlements of Pittington, which Bishop William of St Calais (1083–93) granted to their successors, the Durham Benedictines. From the Prior's Hall at Pittington Hall Garth, adjacent to the church and rebuilt several times, they farmed the estate. Prior Hugh

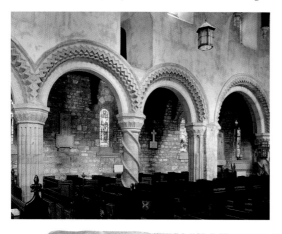

de Darlington built a timber-framed camera (residence) here in 1258, with accommodation for monks, a resident bailiff, stables, dairy, kitchen and other offices. Prior William de Ebchester demolished the hall in 1450, replacing it in stone, with ornate plasterwork and costly hangings. Manorial courts met here and priors made it a summer residence. Hugh Whitehead, the last prior (1524–40), rebuilt the complex within its walled courtyard.

At the dissolution of Durham Priory this, with the estate, was assigned to the 10th Prebendal Stall and leased to tenants. After 1580, the lessee built a new house, buying stone from the demolished priors' camera. The remains were removed during the building of the 19th-century vicarage.

St Laurence's Church

The dedication suggests early origins. St Wilfred brought *brandeis* (cloth strips which had touched the Saint's bones) from the Pope to the King of Northumbria in AD 667. Laurence, a Roman deacon, refused to surrender church treasures during Valerian's persecution, producing instead the poor and sick in his care as his 'treasures'. The west window depicts his martyrdom by burning in AD 258.

There is a 10th–11th-century sundial (lacking a gnomon) on the exterior south wall. Its five lines divided daylight hours into six. The midday line has a cross-bar and is flanked by two on each side with dots at two-thirds of their lengths. The five lines end in squares, an arrangement reminiscent of primitive systems with stones around a central post in the ground.

The plain sandstone font-bowl under the tower is just pre-Conquest. Replaced in 1808 by a pewter basin on a wooden pillar, it was sold in 1809 for a cattle trough, but restored in 1885.

In 1847, the Dean and Chapter offered Pittington the Cathedral's shell font of 1663 erected by Bishop John Cosin. Realising the mistake, its return was requested in 1935, and effected after some opposition from the parish. A richly carved oak cover of tabernacle work cost five shillings in 1628, and formerly hung over the font. The church was broken into several years ago and the font cover was stolen.

The early church, with its small square chancel and high, aisleless nave twice the chancel's size, had small, deeply splayed windows, still visible above the later arcading, and similar to those at St Giles' church *c.* 1112.

▷ **Pittington church interior**: the 12th-century nave arcade

◁ **Memorial to Christian, Bishop's architect**

▲ **Pittington church**: Part of a 12th-century series of frescoes in St Laurence's church illustrating the life of St Cuthbert

▲ **Above: Cuthbert's consecration as Bishop** by Archbishop Theodore

▶ **Right: Cuthbert's vision**, during a meal with Abbess Aelfleda at Osingadun. He saw a Whitby brother die falling from a tree and his soul being carried up to heaven

Two, above the north aisle's west end, contain 12th-century paintings in true fresco by the painter (or his associate) of the figures and draperies behind the Cathedral Galilee's north altar. Survivors of a series depicting St Cuthbert's life, one shows his consecration by Archbishop Theodore, with six other bishops and Ecgfrith, King of Northumbria, looking over his shoulder. The other illustrates Bishop Cuthbert's vision, during a meal with Abbess Aelfleda at Osingadun, of a Whitby brother dying after falling from a tree, and his soul being carried to heaven. Only central yellow lines remain of the tree; its branches and leaves have faded. Many other paintings survived until destroyed in 19th-century 'restoration'. These were covered by a west gallery. On its removal the enlightened vicar, Dr Miller (1822–54), rescued them from damage by workmen.

The nave's north arcade, of highly enriched transitional work, c. 1170, pierces the earlier north wall. Its arches, with chevron moulding on the inner side supported by alternate pillars of spiral and fluted design developed from Durham Cathedral patterns, resemble and pre-date those of its Galilee, built in 1174–5 by Richard de Wolveston, called 'the Engineer', holder of land in Pittington and Newton, who died c. 1182. The Pittington arcade seems to be his and, as a devotee of St Cuthbert, he probably commissioned the frescos.

As chief architect to Hugh of Le Puiset (Bishop of Durham 1154–95), he built also in 1170 the west part of Norham Keep, probably the Constable's Hall at Durham Castle, with its magnificent doorway, and, between 1170–74, Bowes Castle Keep for Henry II.

His successors as the Bishop's architects were William the engineer, and Christian the mason, who held lands in South Sherburn and is buried here. His grave cover, wider at the top than the bottom, of Frosterley or Stanhope marble which had once been in the church, was rescued from the churchyard and now lies at the east end of the south aisle. The two-line Latin inscription means:

> *One bearing the name of Christ is buried in this grave.*
> *Let him who beholds the grave commend him with a*
> *prayer to Christ.*

An original, smaller, tower was contemporary with the north arcade. North-west angle quoins exposed on the north of the tower are characteristic Norman work. The present tower arch on pointed boutells indicates the earliest Early English period for its enlargement, with the pointed windows the second stage, and the north semi-octagonal stair turret. The top stage with embattled parapet is Perpendicular work. The west window of 1585 contains later glass depicting the martyrdom of St Laurence on a gridiron. The tower was buttressed on the south wall in 1609. In the belfry, three medieval bells in an oak bell-frame (probably original) are inscribed:

+ *Sca maria ora pro nobis* (St Mary pray for us)
+ *Sca trinita unus deus miserere nobis* (Holy Trinity one God pity us)
+ *Sancta marineta* (perhaps meant for St Margaret: a bad cast with other letters and traces of a date).

The first two bear the bell-founder's mark: three bells in a shield and may be that of Richard Pette.

Further Additions Before 1250

The north arcade left an eastern respond (half pier) anticipating an extension: a chantry chapel outside the chancel's north wall with responds for a future open arch there, and opened to the north aisle by removing its east wall. A new long chancel was added east of the earlier one, which now became part of the nave with its north wall replaced by the completed Early English arch to the chantry.

Next, the south doorway was widened. Its round arch was moved later in building the south aisle, and again at its rebuilding. It is still used.

The south aisle followed in about 1220, matching the lengthened north aisle but with pointed arches, and the former chancel's wall was taken down. On the north side, the fifth arch was replaced (but leaving responds and capitals) by another to match the south arcade. At the south aisle's east end stood St Katherine's altar, for which Symon de Hawthorne and his wife Matilda left land to support a chantry priest.

Another chantry, St Mary the Virgin, was added later outside the new chancel's north wall and opening from it through two arches. Their pillars and responds had octagonal capitals enriched with foliage *en crochet*, similar to work in the Cathedral's Nine Altars (planned by Bishop Poore who died in 1237, and completed soon after 1278) and probably from the same source. This and St Katherine's chantry had the same priest from 1419. When chantries were dissolved in 1547 it became a vestry; in 1624 a fireplace was inserted; and by 1784 it was demolished and its arches walled up. Later the remains of the carved foliage were re-used in the north aisle.

The 19th Century

An 1816 engraving depicts a north door with a square frame and a late medieval pointed door head. Two steps descend into the north aisle, at that time paved to cover the pillar bases, suggesting much-risen outer and inner ground levels. A plan of 1835 shows a large west gallery (the population had risen with local coal mining), a vestry below in the north-west corner, and the font in the central aisle at its west end. The chancel, with two former north chantry arches walled up and a south priest's door, contained 'open sittings', a survival of the post-Reformation moving of communicants here from the nave at the Prayer of Humble Access; the three east lancet windows remained, but two early round-headed south windows had been blocked *c*. 1807 and one of 'churchwarden's Gothic' substituted. All the nave windows had similar replacements.

Ignatius Bonomi designed alterations in 1846–7. The 12th-century chancel and chancel arch were demolished and rebuilt to lengthen the nave by adding another eastern bay on each side. To do this, both north and south 12th-century responds were moved a bay further east; the 13th-century arch from the north side was added to the south side, which it matched, and on the north side two new round arches were built with a new central pillar. The clerestory was also new.

The south aisle was rebuilt from its foundations, the 14th-century porch rebuilt, and its Norman doorway renovated. The north aisle was partially reconstructed, three Norman-style windows replacing two pointed ones and the north doorway, with two more

Kelloe, St Helen: the exquisite early 12th-century cross, probably sculpted in France, and once brilliantly coloured and gilded, stands against the sanctuary's north wall. Nine cavities may have held jewels or crystal-covered relics, the central one in the cross-head being wood from the 'true cross'. Three panels depict: Constantine's dream; Helen, with book or reliquary, beside Constantine carrying a cross; and Helen (sword in hand) with Judas the Jew (holding spade) finding three crosses. The true cross is revealed when its touch revives one of the corpses buried nearby

further east, one imitating 13th-century style; and at the east end, Bonomi re-used the crocket capitals from the demolished north chapel. Outside, two surviving vertical slit windows about 4 inches wide and with deep inner splays just above ground level were blocked and made invisible inside the church. The ground level has risen and their position relates to a formerly lower nave floor.

North of the chancel a new vestry with a north outer door was added, with an organ bay on its west side.

Later Additions

The chancel screen of 1893 is by W. S. Hicks who designed lengthened aisles in 1897–8. In 1905 the now short chancel was extended eastward, heightened, and furnished (also by Hicks) with the intention to imitate late medieval arrangements. Robed choirs in parish churches became fashionable in the 19th century, copying cathedrals, hence a new organ, carved oak stalls for clergy and choir with panelling and bosses, sedilia against the sanctuary wall, an ancient credence table (perhaps from a former chantry) built into the south side, and elaborate pinnacled reredos with carved figures were introduced. The Lord's Prayer and Commandments were added.

Once removed to the churchyard from a former chantry, the recumbent effigy of *c*.1280 in the north aisle is of a knight in coat of mail and surcoat. His bassinet has the visor down with a horizontal slit for sight. His right hand holds an unsheathed cross-hilted sword with its raised blade partly covered by the shield in his left hand. Right of his crossed legs lies a small dog, and his mailed feet rest on an animal (a dragon?). The shield's armorial bearings are badly weathered, but were a fesse between three popinjays, arms of the Fitz Marmadukes, Lords of Horden in the adjacent Easington parish, and used also by the Lumleys and Thwengs. Beside the font, an early 13th-century coped grave cover about 12 inches long has two toy swords for nobly-born infant twins. Nearby are other children's grave covers, one ornamental with a dentelle border and a galaxy of stars at the foot, besides fragments of Norman corbels and carved stones.

Kelloe and Coxhoe

For Kelloe, about 5 miles south-east of Durham, take the A117. At Coxhoe traffic lights, turn left into the B6291. In about ¹/₂ mile bear right for Kelloe. A drive on the right leads to the site of Coxhoe Hall, now a picnic area. Pass through Kelloe for the church standing on low ground to the right by the beck.

Twenty-six of the seventy-four men killed in Trimdon Grange Colliery on 16 February 1888 lie buried beside their memorial in the extension churchyard.

St Helen's Church

St Helen's Norman tower is of three stages, has single belfry lights and two 12th- and 13th-century sweet-toned bells still in use. One is inscribed *Nomen meum Johannes est* 'My name is John'.

Enter by the south porch and early Norman doorway. The Norman north door is blocked. North and south blocked round-headed windows, visible externally, lit a former west gallery. The Norman nave has windows in later Perpendicular style; the Early English chancel has original lancets, with east and south windows of the Decorated period.

The north bay of the nave was St Mary's chapel or Pity Porch, so-called from a dedication to Our Lady of Pity – Mary at the cross when Jesus' body was removed. It was entered through a pointed arch and half a round one until the 18th century. In 1347, John Fitz Henry de Kellaw and his sister Elizabeth provided lands in Morden to support two chantry priests and Thornley lands for a third: hence its other name, the Thornley Porch. In the 19th century, it became a pew with a ceiling.

Joan, the last of the Kellaw family, married John Fossour. Fossours lived here until the 17th century, moving to Harbourhouse, granted them by Richard Kellaw, Bishop of Durham 1311–16. Their last heir, Basil Fossour, married Anne Tempest, and died without issue. John Tempest bought Kelloe. It passed to his nephew, Sir Henry Vane-Tempest and on his death in 1813, to Lady Frances Vane.

Against the sanctuary's north wall stands a beautiful Norman cross of fine greenish-grey sandstone, once brightly painted, depicting Helen finding the 'true cross'. This object of devotion on the pilgrim road to Durham is the most outstanding of its period in the north. It has affinities with early 12th-century sculpture in France, but its standing figures wear robes with folds in late 12th-century style, which dates the cross. During restorations in 1854 it was found, built into the chancel wall in two parts, lacking only part of the nimbus of the cross head. In the top panel on the shaft, an angel with a scroll (originally lettered) points the reclining Emperor Constantine to the wheel crosshead inscription: IN HOC VINCES 'In this conquer'; the second panel portrays Constantine holding a cross and St Helen, his wife, carrying a reliquary; in the third panel, Helen (with drawn sword) shows Judas the Jew (with spade) where to dig. They uncover two swathed corpses with crosses (perhaps the thieves crucified with Christ). One is revived by touching Christ's cross, thus confirming its identity, by raising a right hand in blessing. Nine cavities probably held jewels or crystal-covered relics; the central one in the cross head would contain a fragment of wood believed to be from the 'true cross' found by St Helen.

The medieval tomb-lid nearby is carved with a foliated cross. On the nave's south side, a modern window depicts the Good Samaritan.

Elizabeth Barrett Browning

On the south wall, a marble slab is inscribed:

> *To commemorate the birth in this parish of Elizabeth Barrett Browning, who was born at Coxhoe Hall, 6th March, 1806, and died at Florence, 29th July 1861. A great poetess, a noble woman, a devoted wife. Erected by public subscription, 1897.*

Kelloe remembers her annually on the date of her death, actually in June, not July!

The Burdons, earlier of Coxhoe Hall, built a gallery (since removed) across the tower arch in 1758; above it now hangs Charles II's handsome coat of arms, *c.* 1680. Below, in the 18th-century shell font, originally painted red, Elizabeth and her brother Edward (born 26 June 1807) were both baptised on 10 February 1808. The parish register records her as 'first child and daughter of Edward Barrett Moulton Barrett of Coxhoe Hall, Native of St James, Jamaica, by his wife Mary, late Clarke, Native of Newcastle-upon-Tyne'.

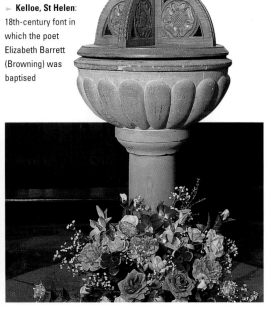

Kelloe, St Helen: the west tower and south porch

Kelloe, St Helen: 18th-century font in which the poet Elizabeth Barrett (Browning) was baptised

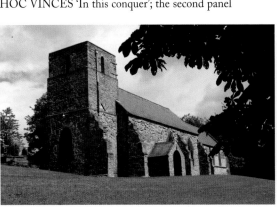

Coxhoe Hall and the Moulton Barretts

In 1794 Charles Moulton, Elizabeth's grandfather, leased Coxhoe Hall. Here his wife brought their four children from Jamaica, after visiting John Graham-Clarke of Kenton Lodge, Newcastle-upon-Tyne, owner of estates in England and Jamaica, a coal mine, flax mills and a brewery. Edward Moulton, at 19, married Mary, first child of Graham-Clarke's second marriage, taking his bride home to Coxhoe Hall. Their first three children were born there before they left for Herefordshire in 1809.

In 1798, Edward and his brother Samuel inherited the estates of their maternal grandfather, Edward Barrett, adding the surname Barrett to their own. Edward believed his family cursed because its massive wealth was derived from slave labour, a view his daughter shared. From this developed his excessively possessive attitude to his family, especially Elizabeth.

Coxhoe Hall, facing south across a landscaped park, and built in 1725 on the site of a 13th-century manor house, contained exceptionally fine plasterwork, probably by the Italian, Joseph Cortese. It passed in 1817 to Anthony Wilkinson, and in 1850 to Thomas Wood, whose descendants sold the estate to East Hetton Colliery Company (probably for underlying coal). The house stood empty until 1939 when it was commandeered for army use and later for Italian prisoners of war. Afterwards, squatters took over and vandalism followed. In 1947, it passed to the National Coal Board which declared it unsafe through mining subsidence, and demolished it in August 1952. In 1983, Durham City Council bought the site, which is now being landscaped for public access.

Ludworth Tower

Take the B1283 through Sherburn and at the top of Sherburn Hill turn right for Shadforth. One mile beyond the village, the ruin of Ludworth Tower rises on the left, with a picnic area.

Ludworth, originally the property of the de Ludworth family, passed in 1411 to the Holden family who built the present tower as the south-west part of an extensive manor house, now vanished.

Ludworth Tower:
the west wall with
remains of basement

Bishop Langley granted Thomas Holden licence to crenellate and fortify it in 1422. Originally, outside steps led to the first floor entrance to the hall, from which the vaulted basement (probably used for secure storage) had its only access. A large part of the tower fell in 1890 and all that remains is part of the basement and, above, the west wall. It stands to a height of three storeys, with fireplaces on two, window openings, the remains of a garderobe and traces of a newel stair in the north-west corner. The present 19th century inclosure road cuts across the site on the south where it slopes steeply to Shadforth Beck. The medieval village was deserted about 1450.

Beaurepaire

For Beaurepaire, leave Durham by the A690. At Neville's Cross traffic lights, turn right on to the A167. At the Pot and Glass, turn left down Toll House Road for Bearpark. The first turn on the right is signposted Bearpark Colliery. After 1/4 mile, turn sharp right by a former chapel (now an organ builder), following the road where it bends left to a colliery tip. After 200 yards, leave the road and turn right down an unmade track. Continue for 1/2 mile, following the colliery tip on the right. After many bends, the track drops into the River Browney valley and Beaurepaire can be seen on the hillside on the right. Park on the flat ground at the junction of the track and the old railway line.

Beaurepaire, a favourite residence of Durham's medieval priors, lay central to a large park. Durham Priory acquired its nucleus c. 1195, made additions 1242–67, and emparked it by a ditch and bank with a timber fence. The park, at first used for cattle, included a 400-acre wood, and was further extended. After Bishop Anthony Bek (1283-1310) broke down the fences and drove out the game during a dispute with Prior Hoton, stone walls replaced first the northern fences and later others.

When Prior Bertram de Middleton resigned in 1258, Beaurepaire and other property was granted for his maintenance. He built here a camera (residence) with a chapel, used by later priors as a country retreat. Its estate, with barns and granaries, developed as a stud farm. The Durham monks had annual summer entertainment here, walking out across the fields with tin picnic plates and mugs.

Edward I was received here in 1296. The Scots, under Robert Brus, devastated the county in 1315, surrounded the park, looted the chapel, carried off furnishings in the prior's cart and drove away 60 horses and 120 cows besides young cattle. The prior and resident monks escaped with difficulty.

Edward II was here in 1318; and Edward III came in 1327, 1333 and 1335.

◄ **Beaurepaire**: ruins of the Prior's manor house
▲ **Brancepeth Castle**: exterior, showing, left, the Baron's Hall

Before the Battle of Neville's Cross on 16 October 1346, King David (Brus) of Scotland's army camped in the park, causing much damage. Afterwards, Prior Fossour undertook extensive repairs and made additions. An inventory of 1464 lists a chapel, outer and inner chambers, hall, buttery and kitchen.

Hugh Whitehead, last Prior and first Dean of Durham, repaired and refurbished Beaurepaire, using it frequently and probably adding a gateway and the great south dormitory window. Until the Civil War, later deans used it occasionally, the last being Dean Hunt (1620–38), when there was only a large useless hall, a dining-room, and three or four other small rooms. In 1640, Scottish rebels damaged part of the buildings and in 1644, 'quite destroyed them'.

Dean Granville's 1684 survey lists both contemporary and former apartments and gardens:

a hall, two passages near the hall, one large kitchen and ovens in it, a back room adjoining on the west end of the kitchen, a dining-room, a great room leading to the chapel called the dormitory, some arches and two rooms above the arches, a chapel and a room under it, three rooms, or two at least called the prior's chamber, and the western room thereof called the prior's lodgings, a little room adjoining the prior's chamber, a staircase and vaults under all and every the lower or floor rooms of the said mansion house, excepting the hall and kitchen and the room aforesaid adjoining the kitchen. And at Beaurepaire aforesaid, there formerly have been belonging to the said manor house several courts and gardens that were walled about, and also sundry outhouses now wholly dilapidated.

By 1787 there remained only the chapel at the south end, a long east-west building at the north, and a long north-south building connecting them. The rest was 'ruinous and confused'. In 1820 only the chapel and the adjoining gable still stood; but by 1846 the chapel was also a ruin.

Further collapses of stonework continued until, in 1979, the city of Durham accepted guardianship to save and consolidate what remained. Emergency work began in March 1980. Archaeologists working under Durham University Excavations Committee followed.

Excavations revealed the lower part of the dormitory's tall south gable and its undercroft, with windows having original 13th-century filleted roll moulding and 16th-century narrowing. The jamb of an upper-floor mid-13th century trefoil-headed doorway has a slot for the beam securing the private door to the prior's apartments to the west. Their basement (possibly for storage) had a western passage. On its west wall is a small chamber with a sub-basement, beyond which a narrow channel with openings at each end served the garderobe above.

The dormitory's south-east corner led to Prior Bertram's beautiful first-floor chapel, with its interior lofty arcade of blank pointed arches divided by shafts with moulded capitals, bands and bases.

The excavated northern buildings had been adapted later for agricultural use. Other remains, as yet unexcavated, lie to the north and east beneath farmland.

Brancepeth

Brancepeth lies 6 miles south-west of Durham on the A690, left and right of which is the attractive 18th–19th-century estate village. To the left, the tree-lined street ends in park gates. Beyond them, the castle stands on the right and St Brandon's church can be seen ahead.

The Castle

Before entering, it is rewarding to walk round the outside, noting the curtain walls with sentry walks and turrets with original work on the west side.

Originally a military stronghold, the castle overlooks the steep ravine of Stockley Beck on the south-west and was moated on the north and east. Here, the moat later became a lake, now dry. Across the beck, the medieval bridge, rebuilt and gothicised, carried the old main road past the castle to the church and ancient village, removed when the park was created.

Brancepeth had a castle by the 12th century, when the Durham monk Reginald wrote of a poor man released from imprisonment here by St Brandon's intervention. The Bulmers owned Brancepeth, besides the Yorkshire lands and castles of Sheriff Hutton, until Emma de Bulmer, daughter and heiress of Bertrand de Bulmer

Brancepth Castle: courtyard

(and widow of Peter de Valoignes) married Geoffrey Neville in 1174. The earliest surviving work is by Ralph Neville, 1st Earl of Westmorland, grandfather of Warwick the King-maker, and Marshall of England from 1399 until his death in 1425. The Nevilles also owned Raby but preferred Brancepeth.

A 16th-century description (the earliest) records two courtyards: one largely bounded by a moat with three lodging towers and three for ornament; the second with a pleasure garden entered by a great tower bearing a lion rampant. Ralph Neville, 4th Earl of Westmorland (1523–49), had just added new work.

The Rising of the North probably began here in 1569, and Charles, the last earl, forfeited his estates to the Crown. In 1613 James I granted Brancepeth to Robert Carr, having made him Baron Brancepeth and Earl of Somerset. Carr's steward's survey describes fine stained glass windows from Normandy with imagery and coats of arms and, in the gallery, portraying the life of Christ.

In 1615, accused of poisoning Sir Thomas Overbury, Carr was imprisoned and in 1629 the Brancepeth property was granted in trust for sale to certain London citizens, who conveyed it, in 1633, to Lady Middleton, Abraham Crosselis and John Jones. In 1635, the British Navy's first three-decker ship, *Sovereign of the Seas*, was built at Woolwich from 1,400 trees felled from the West Wood, across Stockley Beck, south of the castle. The estate was sold in 1636 to Ralph Cole of Newcastle (grandson of a Gateshead blacksmith) in trust for his son, later Sir Nicholas Cole, who made it his home. His son and heir, Sir Ralph, patron of the fine arts and pupil of Van Dyck, became impoverished by keeping Italian painters at Brancepeth.

For £16,800, with a £500 annuity for himself and £200 to his wife if she survived him, he sold Brancepeth in 1701 to Sir Henry Bellasys, whose daughter in the ballad awaited Bobby Shafto of Whitworth Hall across the park. Three Bellasys generations lived here until, in 1774, Sir William's only daughter left the castle and its estates (over 4,600 acres) to her relative, the Earl of Fauconberg. He sold them almost immediately to John Tempest of Wynyard. Sir Henry Vane-Tempest sold

them in 1796 for £75,000 to William Russell, an industrialist and coal-owner who 'wrote to the end of his life like an illiterate labourer' but amassed vast wealth, bought several pocket boroughs (including Saltash and Bletchingly), managed them for the Whigs, and had political connections with Grimsby and Lincoln. His son, Major Matthew Russell, a huge pleasure-seeking man, immense eater and great hunter, married in 1797 Elizabeth Tennyson, aunt of the poet. Although devoted to him, she was in contrast beautiful, charming, refined, a great reader, a writer of verse and deeply religious.

When William Russell died in June 1817, and his widow shortly after, Matthew and Elizabeth moved immediately to Brancepeth and began 'restoration' (major rebuilding), employing John Patterson, the Edinburgh architect, who favoured Norman features but had no architectural knowledge. His huge Norman-style gatehouse with round towers replaced the medieval gateway and portcullis which had been flanked by square towers. He created, at the south-west corner of the courtyard, a porte-cochère before a great entrance hall and grand staircase leading to semi-circular galleries beneath a round skylight, a new dining-room and service wing, the (later-named) Hamilton Tower and a state bedroom. He refitted the vaulted medieval towers: the Neville Tower (south-west) as a drawing-room, exposing a groined vault (again covered) inscribed *Mais Droyte*, and elaborately decorated in the interstices with emblems of the Order of the Garter and the Garter encircling the Neville cross; and the Bulmer Tower (really two towers) (west), with its groined vaults, as the saloon and Baron's Hall. The west end has two side rooms (one a latrine) in the wall thickness.

From the new entrance hall an armour gallery was built inside the courtyard wall, to whose exterior was added the new Russell Tower, containing a state bedroom, replacing a post-medieval building. Through the gallery, the Constable's Tower became the library, connected by a billiard room (above the old stabling) to the Westmorland Tower (east of the gate) fitted as a chapel.

These alterations cost over £120,000. Charles Tennyson (d'Eyncourt from 1835), Elizabeth's brother, acted as 'agent and arbiter', engaging a chef, butler and 12-year-old Emma Maria's governess, and helped Matthew's son William when he was in debt. In return, Matthew got Charles into Parliament. Matthew was MP for Durham for 15 years before he made his maiden speech, urged by Charles. However, when, in September 1819 Charles' baby son died, Matthew's letter of condolence proceeded quickly to discuss armour, historical paintings and other decorations for his 'Baronial Hall'. Stained glass windows designed by Stothard for the Neville Tower each cost £600. The finished castle was opened at Christmas 1820 with lavish festivities.

Elizabeth gave liberally to her poor Tennyson relations, and after Alfred's marriage to Emily Sellwood, on 13 June 1850, offered a honeymoon at Brancepeth. The offer was declined.

In 1828, Emma married Gustavus Frederick Hamilton, eldest son of the 6th Viscount Boyne, to whom the property passed. He was made Baron Brancepeth in 1866. Salvin (Patterson's pupil 1817–21) worked here in 1829 and again in 1864–75 when he refurbished the chapel in memory of Emma Maria, Viscountess Boyne, and was estate architect. He designed the Flagstaff Tower above the porte-cochère and levelled the uneven courtyard to create the present grassy slope.

When Viscount Boyne left the castle in 1922, it became the Headquarters and Museum of the Durham Light Infantry (*see also page 18*). During their occupancy, the property was sold to the Duke of Westminster, and the estate was broken up in the 1960s. Pyrex purchased the castle, using it for research and development until Corning Glass bought out Pyrex and sold the castle into private hands. It was purchased by Mr and Mrs Dobson (of Dobsons Publishers). The castle is undergoing restoration and is, at present, largely unfurnished.

St Brandon's Church

Among trees north-east of the castle stands the church. Beside its dignified gateway a stile, with steps at each side of the wall, has sides built *c.*1665 partly of medieval grave covers; one in the wall is Anglo-Saxon and similar to an example at Escomb. The top has a grating to scrape muddy boots.

There was a Saxon church here, and a rector is recorded in 1085. It was dedicated to St Brandon or Brendon. Born in AD 483 in Kerry, he was one of the twelve apostles of Ireland taught by Finian the Wise at Clonard, and founded Clonfert Abbey on the Boyne. Legend says that he sailed to America, and when Vikings under Eric the Red reached Florida they found Irish-speaking people.

◄ **Brancepeth, St Brandon**: steps of stile into churchyard
► **Brancepeth, St Brandon**: south churchyard: doctor's headstone sculpted with doctor's 'bag' – a basket – and medical instruments

Exterior and tower

Several items of interest should be seen before entering the church: an early sundial (with missing gnomon) on the nave's south-west buttress indicates only service times; an early 13th-century vesica-shaped sculptured stone, let into the north side of the chancel's south-east buttress, represents Christ in Majesty surrounded by symbols of the evangelists (compare another in St Mary-the-Less, Durham); the medieval sanctus bell-cot on the nave's east gable; and, south of the tower, a headstone to Thomas Jonson who died in 1799, with a sculptured basket and medical instruments above an amusing four-line verse.

> '*To the Memory of Thomas*
> *Jonson of This parish Who*
> *Died June The 29 year 1799*
> *Aged 75*
> *What I was once, some may relate*
> *What I am now, is all Men's Fate,*
> *What I shall be, none can explain*
> *Till he that call'd doth call again.*'

The south entrance porch, rarely used, was built in 1892 to commemorate the Reverend R.D. Shafto's forty years as rector.

The tower of three stages is unbuttressed and was begun *c.* 1180. The first floor has small round-headed windows to north and west. The tower, tower arch and the two western arcades of the nave are the earliest part of the present building. The two storeys above have pairs of Early English lancets on each side. Below the parapet several corbels are carved with heads and on one is a shield charged with the Neville saltire.

The belfry has a two-light window, and eight bells were given by the 8th Viscount Boyne to replace an earlier peal of six, three of which were inscribed and presented in 1632 by John Cosin, Bishop of Durham 1660-72, and an active rector here from 1626-40 until he was exiled during the Commonwealth.

The north entrance porch in classical style was added by John Cosin and bears the fret from his coat of arms, and cherubs' heads. It has three doorways with pilasters and Ionic capitals and a curious parapet. The west doorway is now blocked.

The interior

In September 1998 a disastrous fire gutted the interior destroying all the fine woodwork and furnishings installed by Cosin, for which the church was justly famous, as the best preserved 17th-century interior in the north of England. It was the major art-historical loss of the 20th century in the county, yet at the time prompted little more than a minor mention in the local media. Oddly, the brass eagle lectern was found still standing and surveying the wreckage.

Subsequent restoration has been slow and painstaking. In the course of this many archaeological discoveries have been made. Before discussing these, however, it is only right to enumerate what was lost.

Medieval pieces included the front of a fine 14th-century Flemish chest, converted into the front of an altar table by Robert Thompson of Kilburn; the oak altar tomb with effigies of Ralph Neville, 2nd Earl of Westmorland and his second wife Margaret; and two large panelled canopies which had hung above the chancel arch – the lower one is thought to have been brought from the Jesus altar in Durham Cathedral, rescued by George Cliffe, one of the last monks, who became a prebendary and was rector of Brancepeth from 1571 to 1584. The upper one may have been part of the canopy of the Brancepeth rood loft. Most of the woodwork, however, had been installed by John Cosin, who became rector here in 1626 and had furnished the church with magnificent woodwork before 1633, when Newcastle churchwardens with five carpenters visited. His distinctive styles, better known in Durham Cathedral and Castle, and in Auckland Castle chapel, were concentrated here in an almost completely surviving interior deserving detailed attention. His coat of arms, a gold fret on a blue ground, appeared frequently to mark his work.

Other examples of his work may be seen in County Durham, notably in St Peter's chapel in Bishop Auckland Castle and in Sedgefield church, but Brancepeth was without doubt his finest interior. The chancel was almost as he had left it, with pinnacled screen and choir stalls, altar rails, communion table and panelled ceiling. On the north wall was a large blank tablet intended to be his own memorial, for it has been suggested that what he had prepared here was intended as his own mausoleum. In fact, as he became Bishop of Durham, he was buried in Auckland Castle chapel.

Some features survived the fire. The tenor bell fell from the tower, shattering the circular 13th-century font on its Frosterley marble pillar which stood in the tower base. The fragments were retrieved for its restoration. The bells were all removed for conservation and repair, together with the brass eagle lectern.

The brasses in the floor of the south aisle to Thomas Claxton (1403) a knight in armour, c.27 inches long and in the chancel that of Richard Drax (1456), half figure of a priest, c.13 inches long, both survive unharmed.

The recumbent effigy of the 'Peacock of the North' (see below) survived but was damaged and became part of the major conservation work to be undertaken

New discoveries

The losses at Brancepeth have been tragic, but a great deal of new evidence has come to light relating to the earlier history of the church and its medieval development. The nave walls have been shown to be of Saxon date, with massive side-alternate quoining at the west end, typical of c. 700–1000; the west gable of the Saxon church remains intact. The Saxon church was plastered externally, making it stand out white in the landscape. The tower of about 1180 was simply built on the top of the gable. Archaeological evidence shows that the tower replaces a Saxon structure, a western porticus similar to that found at Escomb and elsewhere.

There is some evidence to suggest that transepts may have been added to the nave at around the same time as the tower was built; and twenty or thirty years later the tower was heightened. In the mid-13th century aisles were built and the central sections of the Saxon nave walls were partly taken down to insert the new arcades. The patronage of the Nevilles resulted in several phases of enlargement in the 14th and 15th centuries; the south transept may have been built about 1320, in the Decorated style, as the burial place for Robert, alias 'The Peacock of the North', a turbulent character who slew his rival Richard Fitz Marmaduke, Lord of Horden, on Framwellgate Bridge and was himself killed fighting the Scots at Berwick. The nave may have been always as long as at present. In the later 14th century the chancel was rebuilt as well as the nave aisles, which were now extended to flank the tower. The tower itself was given a new embattled parapet very like that of one of the turrets of the nearby Castle.

Early in the 16th century a chapel was added south of the chancel and east of the south transept, to contain further Neville tombs. Two of the late 14th-century windows from the south side of the chancel were re-set in its external south wall.

One tomb is thought to have been intended as the tomb of Ralph, 3rd Earl of Westmorland, who died in 1523, but in fact was buried at Hornby, in North Yorkshire, another seat of the Nevilles, although his wife Matilda, Countess of Westmorland, was buried here. Her tomb chest with quatrefoil side panels and shields formerly painted with the Neville saltire, was removed in 1876 to the tower base (to make way for an organ chamber), where it was shattered in the fire by a falling bell. Little more than a few fragments of its panelled sides survive. Within the chapel, extensive remains of original wall paintings have been discovered in a scheme of red foliage tendrils. The other tomb chest, uninscribed, was destroyed, leaving only the tomb slab in the floor. The wood funeral helmet, which was once carried on coffins, formerly hung here. It was moved to the north door and perished in the fire.

Beneath this chapel a charnel pit was exposed. It appeared to be the eastern half of a tomb or vault with walls of diagonally dressed ashlar beneath the monument which used to stand under the arch between the chapel and the chancel. Its western half was walled off (by a brick wall). Into the square 'box' provided by the eastern part of the earlier vault, at least six skulls and long bones, were piled, presumably earlier burials from both Westmorland tombs in the chapel, displaced when the Castle or Russell Vault was constructed in the early 19th century for the Russells who owned the Castle from 1796. These have been cleaned and photographed, but not moved in any way. It should prove possible to leave them undisturbed. The Russell coffins were encased in decorated leather and are now sealed beneath the new floor.

There are remains of paintings on the north wall of the chancel, in the area which had been covered and protected by Cosin's intended funerary tablet. The clerestory of the nave was probably also added by Cosin in 1638, when there is a record of timber being sawn for the roof of the 'middle alley', as well as the north and south porches of the nave. When the clerestory was constructed, a large number of medieval grave covers from both the church and the churchyard were re-used as lintels and to cap the walls. It is these which have provided one of the most significant new discoveries: about 70 have been removed from the walls during restoration work, and a further 30 have been recorded but left in place. The current total of about 100 medieval cross slabs is, so far as is known, the largest collection in England apart from those at Bakewell (Derbyshire) where over 300 were found, but only 120 retained during 19th-century rebuilding.

These cross slabs may have been used as the lids of stone coffins, or simply as grave markers in either the church pavement or, those with signs of weathering, in the churchyard. Each is carved with a cross, often very ornate, and many also bear emblems. Most common are swords, indicating the burial of a man with the right to bear arms; also frequent are pairs of small shears, the badge of the medieval housewife (the equivalent of the modern kitchen scissors); at an earlier period pairs of shears sometimes accompanied women's burials. One fine slab has a pair of much larger shears, as well as a sword, probably indicating that the person buried was a cloth merchant. Other cross slab designs – and this is a particularly exciting element in the Brancepeth discoveries – show traces of a 'code' which we do not as yet fully understand: for instance, there are three small crosses at the upper corners and base of the cloth merchant's slab that my have had some significance in the burial ritual. The slabs are to be displayed in the restored church.

Brancepeth, St Brandon: medieval cross slab with shears denoting a cloth merchant and the sword of a gentleman: one of many medieval cross slabs revealed during restoration work

The north aisle windows are copies of the originals, while those of the south aisle are 19th-century replacements. In the north transept the east window copies the original, but the north window is 19th-century work. Both south transept windows have three lights and are of good Decorated style. The east one looks into the later Neville chapel. All the glass was shattered in the fire.

The north chapel (later a vestry), entered through a pointed arch and original door, has an east two-light square-headed window (above an early exterior string-course terminating in leaf ornament), and a north three-light window under a segmented arch, both earlier than the vestry and reset from elsewhere. From the south wall a hagioscope commands the altar and a stone basin in the west wall drains into the churchyard.

The hagioscopes in either side of the chancel arch were inserted so that worshippers in the aisles could see the altar. The position of the entrance to the rood loft stair can be identified.

At the west end, the replacement of the organ lost in the fire is a magnificent 'Father' Willis pipe organ of the 1870s from the closed Winterton Hospital near Sedgefield, where it was acquired for the new chapel in 1884.

The new clerestory windows are designed with a pattern taken from a 12th-century cross slab found there.

The heat of the fire, which reached 1,200 degrees, had burnt the stonework of the arcades. Steel needles were used to support the clerestory while the columns were replaced. The massive roof timbers fell. The new ceiling is made of ash with a stainless steel roof above.

Croxdale

Croxdale lies about 2 miles south of Durham.
At Sunderland Bridge take a right turning and then
turn left. The entrance gates to the park are immediately
south of Sunderland Bridge. The Hall, gardens,
and medieval chapel are ½ mile further.

Before 1350, Croxdale was the estate of Robert de
Whalton, whose grandchild Agnes, as heiress, took the
estate to the Salvin family of East Yorkshire on her
marriage with Gerard Salvin in 1402. Since then it has
descended through this family in an unbroken line.

Bryan Salvin, who died in 1751, conserved the
extensive woodland which covered a large part of the
estate. Between 1751 and 1758 his son sank coal pits
and built colliery houses in the vicinity, but was careful
to protect the amenities of Croxdale Hall.

The chapelry of Croxdale was originally dependent on

▲ **Croxdale Hall**: south front
▼ **Croxdale old church**: the south side

St Oswald's, with its first recorded incumbent in 1176.
The medieval building has a Norman south doorway
with interesting door furniture and above, a badly
weathered tympanum sculpture with what seems to
represent a Tree of Life. The blocked north door and
chancel arch are probably late 12th-century. There is a
lancet window on the north side and the east window is
of three lights in the Decorated style. Three members of
the Salvin family have been interred in the chancel; and
there is a Salvin memorial cross in Saxon style in the
churchyard. With the coming of mining and the growth
of the colliery village, by an arrangement with the
Church of England, the medieval chapel of Croxdale
ceased to be used except as a school. The Salvins built
the present Croxdale church just off the main road in
exchange for the medieval building which has become
their private property. It was used at first as a school but
later became derelict, with no furniture except an
abandoned long school desk. Recently, seating has been
introduced.

Across the drive, behind a stone wall, stands Croxdale
Hall, built *c.* 1760 for General Salvin, father of the
architect. Its west front of seven bays has a central
doorway with Tuscan columns and a Venetian window
above. The south side, facing a garden, is of five bays,
with a three-bay pediment. There is 18th-century
plasterwork on the staircase and drawing room ceilings.
Beside the drive on the north side there is an older wing,
which was adapted by the 18th century by the addition of
two large bows with Venetian windows. Those on the east
were blocked in 1807 by the insertion of a 'thinly Gothic'
private Roman Catholic chapel, with an altar painting,
The Mourning of Christ by Maria Cosway. The chapel is

▲ **Croxdale Hall**: gardens, lake and orangery
► **Chaytor family of Butterby**: Elizabethan memorial
in St Oswald's church, Durham

Norman owners because of its beautiful seclusion by the River Wear. The 1-acre site of the former manor house, entered by a bridge and arched gateway, with its offices, domestic chapel and gardens, was low in the valley, and defended by a moat, walled but now dry. It was capable of flooding to a depth of 15 feet. In the 16th century it passed to the Chaytor family, one of whom, Christopher Chaytor sometime retainer of the Duke of Somerset, died in 1592 aged 98, and is buried at St Oswald's. His fine memorial is on the nave north wall (*see page 21*). Re-used 12th-century architectural fragments have been found at Butterby; and in the 18th century, in a stone coffin in the moat, was reputedly found a coat of mail with a cap of chain work quilted in canvas, a breast plate and buckles. In 1827 a lady's gold ring was also found here. In a nearby field a number of stone coffins were found, indicating the probable site of a chapel.

About 2 miles from Durham, in the middle of the river, a strong saline spring rises from a fissure in the rock, and within a few yards, on the Durham bank, a spring strongly impregnated with sulphur long ago attracted walkers.

used by Roman Catholics of the neighbourhood who lack a local church.

The gardens extend over 9 acres. West of the house, a long terrace, sheltered on the north side by a brick wall with fruit trees, flower beds and an orangery, skirts a sloping lawn beside a large fish pool or lake, with views of the open country beyond.

Before 1813, the neighbouring estate of Burn Hall (west of the A167) was sold to Bryan John Salvin, younger son of William Salvin of Croxdale Hall, with opportunities for conserving the landscape and river banks. He commissioned the building of the present Burn Hall mansion and died in 1842. When Marmaduke Henry Salvin died in 1924, Burn Hall was offered for sale by his trustee, Major Salvin of Croxdale, a Roman Catholic. He sold it to the Mill Hill Fathers (St Joseph's Society for Foreign Missions) to found a junior seminary where boys would be encouraged to become missionary priests. St Joseph's College opened in 1926, but closed in 1972 when junior seminaries fell from favour. The Mill Hill Missionaries left Burn Hall on 29 August 1995 and Burn Hall was sold to a housing trust for conversion into ten private residences.

The very fine byre and long barn of 1786 designed by Sir John Soane as part of the Home Farm buildings, which are no longer part of the estate, have been retained. The splendid cow-house has a central pavilion with high arched entrance and pediments, flanked by diagonally placed wings, each with three arches, and terminating in small pavilions with pyramid roofs. It was converted for occupation by four missionary priests but is now in private hands.

Before 1834 William Thomas Salvin of Croxdale bought Butterby, the ancient Beautrove, so-called by its

Bishop Auckland: Auckland Castle and the Bishop's Park

Auckland Castle lies at the east end of the Market Place. It became the only residence of the bishops of Durham when Bishop Van Mildert, last of the prince-bishops, gave up Durham Castle in 1832 to found Durham University. Its massive gateway, crowned by a pinnacled clock turret, was designed *c.* 1760 by Sir Thomas Robinson for Bishop Richard Trevor. The Elizabethan-style lodge within is a century later.

Durham bishops probably had a residence at Auckland before the Norman Conquest. A 10th-century grant of 'two Aclits' to the church of Durham refers to West Auckland and St Andrew Auckland (South Church), which had a pre-Conquest church. Bishop Auckland grew up later beside the episcopal manor house, where Bishop Hugh of Le Puiset built a hall about 1183. It was never fortified; but Bishop Hatfield called it a *castrum* (fortified building) in 1346, when the English army camped in the park on the night before the Battle of Neville's Cross.

A north gatehouse, built by Bishop Skirlaw (1388–1406), was convenient for access from St Andrew Auckland, a mile to the south-east; it may have led into a courtyard behind the gallery wing called Scotland (left of the present entrance), erected to lodge Scottish hostages sent occasionally by the king into the bishop's custody. (Skirlaw also built Auckland Bridge, on the Wolsingham road.)

The long straight drive, beside a low arcaded wall, passes the south end of the north-south wing to the recessed three-arched crenellated gateway to the Castle itself. It was designed by James Wyatt for Bishop Barrington whose coat of arms, with those of the diocese, decorates the centre arch. The drive terminates in the beautiful Bishop's Park.

The medieval Castle has been extended and adapted. After the Civil War, Parliament confiscated and sold it as church property c. 1650 to Sir Arthur Haslerigg for £6102 8s. 11d. An inventory made for him lists courts, yards and gardens totalling 6 acres within an encircling wall still partly embattled. He demolished the chapel to re-use the materials for a new mansion in the grounds, probably never finished. Other buildings fell into decay. At the restoration of the monarchy, church property was returned to its owners and Haslerigg was sent to the Tower.

Bishop John Cosin (1660–72) restored the Castle; but Bishop Barrington (1791–1826) with his architect James Wyatt made subsequent alterations.

The entrance

Bishop Barrington's ornate entrance porch of 1794 leads into a vestibule created by Bishop Cosin to link the chapel with the domestic buildings.

Auckland Castle gateway:
St Peter's chapel opposite

The State and Domestic apartments

The Entrance or Gentlemen's Hall

The oldest surviving part of the north-south two-storey wing built by Bishop Antony Bek (1283–1312, whose short sword is still at the Castle) is the entrance hall left of the vestibule. It was restored by Bishop Cosin, whose coat of arms appears in the window glass; but the architect James Wyatt transformed it for Bishop Barrington (1791–1826) by removing the west wall to insert his elegant staircase, and covering the early massive oak beams with an ornate false gothic ceiling. Shields bearing the coats of arms of English dioceses hang high on the walls. Former bishops left items here, including the stuffed snowy-owl which failed to discourage the many bats in the chapel.

To the left, in the great kitchen, where massive pillars support the great chamber above, a colourful exhibition tells the story of St Cuthbert and the history of Durham Diocese.

The staircase divides after the first flight, the right branch mounting to a window overlooking the Wear valley and the route of the original entrance road. The landing leads past a large tapestry, and the head of the left stair, to the ante-chamber and Throne Room, created from the 76 ft-long medieval great common room.

The ante-chamber

In this elegant octagonal room, visitors once awaited an audience with the bishop. Over a doorway on the left, leading to the Victoria wing (occupied by Queen Victoria when travelling north), hangs a portrait of Bishop Thomas Wolsey (1523–80), who never visited his diocese. George Richmond's two pastel-chalk drawings of Montague Villiers and his wife hang in this room: he was bishop only for the year 1860. On the right, the large window looks towards Scotland and the kitchen garden, where the right-hand south-facing wall once carried heating pipes to ripen peaches. Slender double doors with fine brass work lead into the Throne Room.

Auckland Castle: St Peter's Chapel: ceiling with Bishop Cosin's coat of arms

The Throne Room

At the south end, the central arch of an elaborate plaster screen frames the bishop's throne. Above are the arms of the diocese impaled with those of Bishop Barrington, surmounted by a ducal coronet and mitre with a crook and sword, signifying the temporal, spiritual and pastoral office of the prince-bishops.

Here, as the monarch's representative, bishops received the sons and daughters of northern nobility, to save the long and hazardous journey to London to be presented at court. James Wyatt tinted the south-facing Gothic windows pink and green 'to make the ladies appear less pale in the bright sunlight'.

Former bishops' portraits look down from the walls. Bishop John Cosin, restorer of Auckland Castle, hangs to the right of the fireplace, while on the left is Bishop Van Mildert (who died in 1836), last of the prince-bishops. A former bishop brought the marble tops of the two gilt tables flanking the fireplace from Thomas Becket's shrine at Canterbury. A carved door to the right of the throne leads to another state room.

The 16th-century addition

Bishop Thomas Ruthall (1509–22) began to extend Bek's buildings southwards, with an oriel of two storeys next to his great chamber. It contains the long dining-room above the former servants' hall, made into the library in the early 20th century. Bishop Tunstal's device of a curry comb with bird supporters (for horse grooming) decorates the ceiling of the raised window bay, and Bishop Ruthall's coat of arms appears over the lower oriel. Next, over the stone entrance hall, is the chamber later known as the King Charles Room. Bishop Tunstal (1529–59) completed the work by 1530.

The dining-room

This apartment is almost the same size as the Throne Room. Bishop Trevor's coloured coat of arms is in the centre of the moulded ceiling of 1760. The inlaid African ebony table extends to four times its present size; and Bishop Barrington's coat of arms decorates the scrolled tops of the rosewood chairs. Wyatt designed the three side-tables. Thirteen priceless paintings of 1640, each 8 feet tall and by the Spaniard Francesco Zurburán, represent Jacob and his twelve sons. Bishop Trevor bought them for £124 after pirates captured them on their way to South America.

The King Charles Room

Charles I slept here when travelling to and from Scotland, the last time as a prisoner being taken to London for trial and execution.

This is the family dining-room on special occasions, and is not usually shown to visitors. The fireplace, in the Grinling Gibbons style, has a charming central sculpture of two children and a bird's nest. The rococo ceiling carries Bishop Trevor's badge: a dragon sitting on a bishop's hat. He bought Vecchio's *Judgement of Solomon*, the copy of Paolo Veronese's *Wedding Feast at Cana in Galilee*, and the four evangelists, painted on wood by G. Lanfranco, in the corners.

The Chapel

A chapel existed by 1271, but Bishop Antony Bek (1283–1312) is said to have built a new one of two storeys. Probably he added to the existing chapel the upper storey known as the high chapel. It stood parallel to the south side of the great hall until *c.* 1650, when Haslerigg, the Commonwealth lay owner, demolished it, intending to use its materials to build a new house, possibly never finished. The original chapel outline is visible in the grass in dry summers.

Bishop Hugh of Le Puiset built the great aisled hall (now the chapel). Four-shafted columns, two of sandstone and two of Frosterley marble, carry the arcades. The east wall had three doorways (now blocked) leading down steps to kitchen, buttery, pantry and other domestic offices. Two blocked doorways in the north wall's eastern bay are visible externally. The lower one was the north entrance to the screens passage, while the higher one led to the musician's gallery above. The dais and high table occupied the hall's west end adjacent to the bishop's private apartments. A central open hearth, with its smoke louvre above, provided heating. The windows of the north and south aisles, and the west end of the nave, are ascribed to Bishop Hatfield (1345–81).

When Bishop John Cosin (1660–71) destroyed Haslerigg's work and restored the property, he spent large sums, especially in converting the great hall into St Peter's chapel, and in connecting it to the main house on the west by a short wing. The outer doors, the ante-chapel door, and the chapel's western screens all display Cosin's distinctive style of woodwork.

Above the north and south arcades he built a high clerestory to give lightness and loftiness, heightening the roof to 64 feet, and raising the floor in black and white marble; he also added the white marble sanctuary steps. Above the Holy Table hung a tapestry (since removed) representing Solomon's meeting with the Queen of Sheba. Cosin's ceiling displays his coat of arms (a gold fret on blue) and the arms of the diocese in gold blue and silver, in alternate squares, painted by Van Eersell who worked also in Durham Castle and Bishop Cosin's Library. The central panel is flanked by cherubs, mitres and eagles. Cosin's coat of arms once also decorated the window glass. He was buried in the central aisle beneath the epitaph he composed.

His successor, Bishop Nathaniel Crewe, gave the Father Schmidt organ (with black and white keys reversed) for the west gallery in 1688. Bishop Van Mildert (1826–36) carried out extensive repairs, marked by his own arms cut occasionally into Cosin's woodwork.

Bishop Joseph Barber Lightfoot (1879–89) restored the chapel, adding a new oak Holy Table with cedar panels; a carved dark

▲ **Auckland Castle: St Peter's Chapel**: one of a series of windows illustrating the history of the church in Northumbria

▼ **Auckland Castle: St Peter's Chapel**: carved bench end

Frosterley marble reredos with oak above; the credence table (part of an ancient altar slab found in the house); the six angels standing on the corbels which supported the roof of the original hall; and the heraldic shields round the walls. Both at the east end and from six windows east of the screen, he removed the inferior glass which had gradually replaced Cosin's original windows. He planned the present windows to describe the spread of the Christian faith from New Testament times, continuing through the Northumbrian saints, and descending to the See of Durham, naming later bishops.

To the chapel re-dedication he invited fifty-seven bishops, recording their names on brass plates flanking the doorway beneath the organ gallery. Lightfoot died the next year and is buried in front of the sanctuary.

Joseph Nollekens' monument to Bishop Richard Trevor (d. 1771) is in the south-west corner of the ante-chapel.

The Bishops' Park

From the three-fold Castle entrance, the long arcaded wall beside the drive continues to the beautifully wooded and undulating Bishops' Park of 800 acres with its excellent picnic areas. The River Gaunless (the 'loiterer') winds across its south side to meet the River Wear just beyond the Castle's outer wall near the Binchester road.

Like the Castle, the park is owned by the Church Commissioners; it is open to the public except for parts leased to local farmers and to Bishop Auckland Golf Club.

Boldon Book (1183) recorded the park where, as in other medieval parks, wild animals were driven within its ditch and paling to be hunted

▲ **Bishops' Park, Bishop Auckland: the deer cote of 1760** with tower on its east side. In its upper room the bishop and his guests could rest during hunting expeditions
► **Chester-le-Street: St Mary and St Cuthbert's church** with the Anker's House left of the tower

for food when needed. Bishop Philip of Poitou had enlarged it by 1200. After the English army camped here on the night before the Battle of Neville's Cross in 1346, and perhaps to repair the depredations of the troops, Bishop Hatfield newly walled it in stone for £40 in 1349. Deer are mentioned in 1394, and Leland wrote of 'fallow dere and wild beasts' in 1587. A 1627 survey records 'wilde kyne with calves and bulls, etc., of all sortes'; and in 1634 they were said to be 'white' and could be 'violent and furious'. All had been exterminated before the Parliamentary Survey of 1647.

At the Restoration, Bishop Cosin re-stocked the park and appointed park keepers; and Bishop Joseph Butler (1750–2) seems to have extended it and rebuilt its ruined walls.

In 1760 Bishop Richard Trevor built a large deer cote (now in the care of English Heritage) with a grassed quadrangle within arcades to shelter fallow deer. The tower on its east side once had an upper room where the bishop and his guests could rest during hunting expeditions. In 1852 there were about 300 deer; and deer roamed the park more recently. Sadly, there are none today.

Chester-le-Street

St Mary and St Cuthbert's Church

The church was built on the site of a Roman fort (*Concangium*) and began as the seat of the Bishop of Lindisfarne from 882. Here, the Congregation of St Cuthbert settled after the Viking raids on the north-east coast, before finally moving to Durham in 995. The present church, where parts of the Saxon nave walls survive above ground and possibly also in parts of the chancel, is otherwise mostly of the 13th century. It contains a remarkable series of fourteen monumental effigies, mostly placed here against the north wall of the nave in the late 16th century by John, Lord Lumley, to commemorate his ancestors.

The Anker's House

The western bay of the north aisle has been walled off to form the two rooms of the Anchorage, or Anker House, one above the other; and two similar rooms, connecting with them, were built outside the aisle. A recluse or anchorite lived here from the 1380s, spending his time in prayer and meditation, the earliest known being John Wessyngton. After the Reformation it became a small almshouse. In 1986, the Anker's House became an attractive museum of the town's history and church treasures from Roman times onwards, receiving honourable mention in the Museum of the Year Awards.

Monkwearmouth

St Peter's Church

Monkwearmouth is now part of Sunderland. Here, on the north bank of the Wear, Benedict Biscop founded a monastery on land granted by Ecgfrith, King of Northumbria, in 675. This was followed by its 'twin' at Jarrow in 684. St Peter's west wall originally had a doorway at its south end (perhaps beside a west altar), blocked when a little later a central door and porch were added, the latter the burial place of Eosterwine (*d*.685), the first abbot appointed by Biscop. The porch has arched openings with baluster shafts decorated with intertwined creatures; above are faint traces of a large figure sculptured in relief. The fourth stage and belfry of the tower are late pre-Conquest.

The church had an eastern apse and north and south porticus (side-chambers of Anglo-Saxon type), but was rebuilt in the 14th century. The north aisle was added in the 13th century and rebuilt and extended in 1874 to meet the needs of a rising population. The Anglo-Saxon monastic site south of the church has been extensively excavated. The Venerable Bede began his monastic life here and the famous *Codex Amiatinus* and other manuscripts were written here. St Peter's became a cell of Durham Priory after the Norman Conquest. St Peter's has a visitor centre displaying excavation finds and a descriptive video.

Monkwearmouth, St Peter's church:
8th-century west tower and porch
with decorated baluster shafts

Jarrow: St Paul's church and Bede's World

The church, the monastic site and Bede's World lie together 10 miles from Newcastle off the A19 (exit at the south end of the Tyne Tunnel).

St Paul's parish church has been used for worship for thirteen centuries. Its chancel was the smaller of two Anglo-Saxon monastic churches on the same east-west axis; and its present nave and north aisle (1866) stand on the site of a larger church, which was decorated richly with early sculpture now on display. The foundation stone is set into the chancel arch facing the present nave. Each May, the church holds an annual lecture on Bede and his times by a distinguished scholar.

The adjacent Anglo-Saxon monastic site on the banks of the River Don has been excavated, its plan laid out, and the later Norman monastic ruins conserved. An excellent model of the Anglo-Saxon monastery may be seen in Jarrow Hall.

Bede's World is a striking new museum designed by award-winning architects. This, and the Georgian Jarrow Hall, display Northumbria's early history and explore the remarkable achievements of the life and times of the Venerable Bede (673–735), the renowned monk, scholar, prolific writer and teacher. He was called the 'father of English historians' from his fame as author of *The History of the English Church and People*. Jarrow, the twin monastery of St Peter's Monkwearmouth, was internationally famous in Bede's day as a centre of Christian learning. Bede's remains lie in Durham Cathedral.

After the Norman Conquest, Jarrow became a cell of Durham Priory.

Gyrwe, Jarrow's name in Bede's day, brings to life the world he knew, with its timber buildings under construction, its farming methods, crops and animals.

◄ **Jarrow, St Paul's**: Anglo-Saxon church, now chancel of the present church
▲ **Jarrow, St Paul's**: later monastic ruins south of the church

Raby Castle

Escomb church: interior looking east

The River Don, once a natural harbour, is landscaped to restore inter-tidal mudflats as a habitat for wading birds.

St Paul's, with its associated sites, is being revived today as a centre of historical, religious and cultural importance. Amenities include a gift shop, restaurant, temporary exhibitions and events, small conference or meeting facilities and free parking.

Raby Castle

Raby, one of the most magnificent medieval castles in the country, is said to be on the site of the Staindrop mansion of King Cnut (995–1036). Bertram de Bulmer (of Brancepeth and Sheriff Hutton) was grandfather of the Norman heiress Isabel Neville, who married the Lord of Raby and gave the name Neville to their descendants. Raby has a distinguished history. Joan Beaumont, John of Gaunt's daughter and the king's sister, was the second wife of Ralph Neville, 1st Earl of Westmorland, the mother of Cicely Neville, the 'Rose of Raby'. Cicely married Richard Plantagenet, Duke of York, and was the mother of Edward IV and Richard III. On 13 November 1569 in the Barons' Hall, the northern nobles and gentry plotted the fatal Rising of the North, when the Crown confiscated the castle and Raby estates. After 43 years under the charge of a Keeper, Sir Henry Vane bought Raby and Barnard, and twice received Charles I at Raby.

The castle has magnificent apartments with fine paintings, furniture and porcelain, and a 14th-century kitchen. There are 10 acres of gardens; and the park of 270 acres (exclusive of enclosed woodlands) contains two herds of deer, one red and the other fallow. Raby is the seat of Harry John Neville, 11th Lord Barnard, who was appointed Lord Lieutenant of County Durham in 1970. He is descended from both the Vanes and the Nevilles.

Escomb Church

One and a half miles west of Bishop Auckland, and built probably between 670 and 690 from Roman stones, Escomb church stands on low ground near the river, in a roughly circular churchyard suggesting possibly a Celtic religious site, followed by thirteen centuries of Christian worship. Do not fail to walk round the outside first, before entering. The church exterior, 36-feet high and narrower at the top, was originally plastered. There was once a western annexe, matching the chancel in size. The austere north side is unaltered Saxon work and contains a rosette from a Roman altar. The blocked north doorway has a single stone lintel and massive 'long and short' stone jambs leaning towards each other.

▲ **Escomb**:
7th-century
Anglo-Saxon
church,
south side
► **Escomb**:
18th-century
gravestone with
symbols of
mortality

A similar blocked doorway led from the chancel into a former Saxon porticus or side-chamber. Beside it, a reversed Roman stone is inscribed LEG VI (the sixth legion). The western annexe and porticus were excavated in 1968. Under the former were burials pre-dating the annexe; and Saxon window glass like that at Jarrow was found on the porticus site. High on the south wall is a Saxon sundial whose three lines mark the hours of prayer; it has a crown above and a Teutonic serpent from Anglian pre-Christian religion curves round the dial.

Entrance is through the south porch, which today houses finds and Saxon carving. The nave has its original five high windows, square-headed on the north and round-headed on the south and in the west gable. The north-east window has a Roman inscription on the right jamb. Once all the windows had horn-covered shutters. The crude font, still used, is shaped for the total immersion of infants. The sanctuary or chancel is entered beneath a tall re-assembled Roman arch with an Irish consecration cross incised beside it, and traces of wall-painting are visible beneath the arch itself. Part of a 9th-century stone standing cross or grave cover stands behind the altar; the right jamb of the blocked north door is carved with Adam and Eve beside the Tree of Life; and the inserted 13th-century south lancet window jamb is a re-used Saxon stone etched similarly to grave memorials at Hartlepool.

In the 13th century two windows were added to admit more daylight: a tall lancet in the chancel, and another

in the nave; the western annexe was demolished, and its stone was re-used to construct the south porch. Its sundial was a 17th-century addition. These, and 19th-century east and west windows and one in the nave, are the only changes to the Saxon building. A perceptive visitor will find a wealth of other detail.

The churchyard contains a number of interesting early headstones.

The church had no known dedication; but a new church dedicated to St John was built on higher ground to serve an increased 19th-century population. This has since been demolished leaving only its graveyard. Recently, the dedication has been transferred to the Saxon church.

Lumley Castle

The castle crowns a hill above the River Wear in pleasant parkland (6 miles north of Durham, 1 mile east of Chester-le-Street and close to the A1(M)). The castle, built in the 14th century with a central courtyard and four great corner towers, incorporates Sir Ralph Lumley's earlier manor house as its west side. The original east entrance, flanked by angle-towers, overlooks the deep ravine of Lumley Beck. Richard Lumley, who became Earl of Scarbrough in 1689, planned alterations for which his son, in 1721, commissioned designs by Sir John Vanbrugh, including fine stuccoed decorations to walls and ceilings. The present earl is no longer resident and the castle was converted to a hotel in 1974.

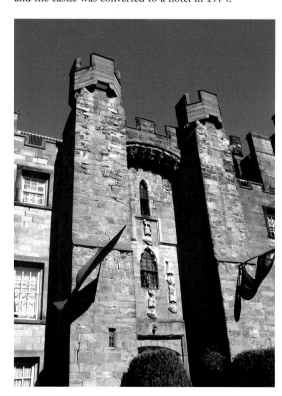

Lumley Castle: the barbican and original entrance

Finchale Priory

Finchale Priory was built on the site of St Godric's hermitage. Godric's life was written by the Durham monk Reginald who knew him personally. He was born in Norfolk about 1086 and early in life became a travelling pedlar. He seems always to have been a wanderer. When about twenty years old he went to Rome and on returning in 1065, sailed as part owner of a vessel trading to North Sea ports in Scotland, Denmark and Flanders. In 1102, in the Mediterranean, he may be identified with 'Guderic, a pirate from the Kingdom of England' who gave a passage to King Baldwin I of Jerusalem from Arsuf to Jaffa. On the return voyage he landed in Spain and made a pilgrimage to Compostela.

After a short stay in England he went to St Gilles in Provence and again to Rome. He then set out, this time taking his mother, for a third visit to Rome.

In 1104 he settled in a lonely place near Carlisle; and then joined a hermit at Wolsingham. He evidently intended to go on pilgrimage again, because while there, he had a vision in which he was told that on his return St Cuthbert would find him a hermitage at a place called Finchale, not yet known to him.

When the hermit died in 1106, Godric set out for Jerusalem. On returning, he settled for a time at Whitby; then he moved to Durham, learned to read at St Mary's in the Bailey, moved to the Hospital of St Giles to hold a minor office, and then to the Cathedral Priory where he found out about Finchale. Bishop Rannulf Flambard gave him leave *c.* 1110 to settle there. It was part of the Bishop's hunting ground.

Initially he settled by the Wear approximately a mile above the priory, moving in 1115 to Finchale itself, then wild and overgrown, liable to flooding and infested with poisonous snakes. He lived at first in a primitive hut roofed with turf, later building a small, rough wooden chapel of St Mary, with living and storage quarters attached. It lay east of the north transept of the later church. In 1138 he was disturbed by marauding Scots under David I.

Godric's growing reputation as a holy man attracted many visitors and about 1150 a second and larger chapel of stone dedicated to St John the Baptist was built for him from their gifts. It measured internally 33 feet six inches by 15 feet 6 inches: its walls still stand about 3 feet high below the present floor level of the quire of the later church which encloses it. From then until his death in 1170 he left Finchale only three times. In later life he had contact with Ailred, abbot of Rievaulx; and with William of St Barbe, Bishop of Durham.

Normally his life was severely ascetic: he wore a hair shirt and coat of mail, and often prayed in cold water up to his neck. He had a deformed hand, probably resulting from Dupuytren's contracture, but believed by contemporaries to be caused by carrying a service book on a thong or cord suspended from his fingers, and regarded as a sign of his sanctity. Eight years before his death he

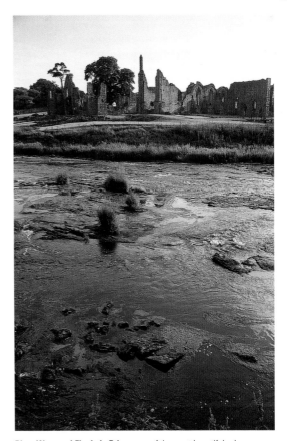

River Wear and Finchale Priory, one of the most beautiful ruins in the country

became confined to his bed in the chapel of St John where he died aged 106. He was buried in a coffin, 5 feet 2 inches long internally, hewn from a single block of stone in a stone-built grave against the middle of the north wall where his bed had stood. A cross in the turf marks the site.

At Godric's death the hermitage and its buildings passed to the Prior and Convent of Durham, who sent two monks, Reginald and Henry, to live there.

Henry Puiset, one of three sons of Bishop Hugh of Le Puiset (1154-1191), founded a monastery at Haswell, near Durham, for Augustinian canons, as a daughter house of Gisborough. They soon moved to Baxtanford (Baxterwood) on the River Browney; but the Durham Benedictines objected to an Augustinian house so near Durham Priory. Henry Puiset was obliged to grant its possessions to Finchale, which was granted to him on condition that he should re-grant it, as a newly founded Benedictine monastery, to Durham which then had the right of appointing the priors. In 1196, Finchale became a cell of Durham, and Thomas the sacrist of Durham became the first prior.

Many pilgrims visited Godric's shrine. The new monastery flourished with its first buildings (whose remains are still visible on the bank of the Wear) on the ordinary domestic pattern, with a hall and solar at the north end.

Godric's chapel of St John the Baptist served the few monks, whose numbers reached only fifteen in 1278.

More formal buildings began *c.* 1237, to be completed nearly at the end of the 13th century. The large cruciform church embraced St John the Baptist's chapel; its high altar was consecrated in 1239; over the crossing a low tower and spire were supported on four cylindrical piers, with a stair to the upper storey in the north-west pier. North and south aisles flanked nave and choir; south of the nave were the cloisters; chapter house and domestic offices occupied the east side, with the dormitory above; there was a refectory of two storeys on the south side; with the adjacent Prior's hall, camera, study, and chapel stretching eastwards parallel with the church choir. East of the north transept was St Godric's chapel with altar, light and a chest for offerings made at his tomb. The aisles and chapel were demolished in 1364 and 1365, perhaps to save costly repairs, leaving the traceries of blocked windows. The nave south aisle served as the north cloister alley. A two-storey vaulted building at the church's south-west angle was probably used by the cellarer.

Later the monks' daily life centred on the large prior's lodging east of the cloister. The hall became their refectory with a serving hatch from the kitchen.

Finchale became a holiday resort for Durham monks. Statutes of 1408 laid down the exact arrangement: basically, there was to be a resident prior with four monks, plus four Durham monks who were to stay for three weeks as visitors, to be replaced by four others, in rotation. Each day, two of the visitors kept the daily round of services, while the other two, apart from

attending mass and vespers, might walk abroad 'religiously and honestly'.

The considerable remains of church, cloister and other buildings from the mid-13th century are in the custody of English Heritage.

Directly aligned with the north transept is a stone 'farmhouse' which has a very fine crown-post roof probably dated to the 14th century. Its high-status first floor rooms suggest that this was a hostel for pilgrims close to St Godric's shrine. Was it linked by a bridge to a gallery inside the church?

Washington Old Hall

The original house was built in the 12th century. The former entrance was from the village green and ran past the east end of the church, where its route may be traced today by faint ridges in the grass of the churchyard. The church and hall site were enclosed by a moat, formed partly by Washington Beck which rose as a spring (the Spout), flowed south to a pond, and continued west of the church and hall buildings before turning sharply eastwards. A ditch, later the churchwardens' responsibility, skirted the mound's east and north slopes, connecting it with the pond. The hall was formerly a courtyard house, with barns, buildings for stabling, a watermill, and lodgings for men-at arms on the west side of the courtyard.

Here, until 1452, lived the descendants of William de Wessyngton, direct ancestor of George Washington, first President of the USA. William de Hertburn (near Stockton in County Durham) was descended from

Washington Old Hall: view from the nuttery. 17th-century manor house incorporating the 12th-century remains of the home of George Washington's ancestors and from which the family derives its name

Washington Old Hall: Great Hall looking west to the two medieval arches with kitchen beyond

eminent forebears and when the Bishop of Durham granted him Washington as his main residence a little before 1180, he changed his name, as was the custom before the introduction of surnames, to that of his new home. Whether he, or predecessors here, built the first house is uncertain. His great-grandson, Sir Walter de Wessyngton II, was one of the 85 knights who fought on the barons' side in Simon de Montfort's rebellion against Henry III, concluded in the Treaty of Lewes in 1264. In September 1304 King Edward I stayed here for several days to transact business on his return from the Scottish Border in the time of the third Sir Walter de Wessyngton and needed accommodation for his retinue. Sir William de Wessyngton fought at the Battle of Otterburn (Chevy Chase) in 1388, but his death in 1399 ended the family's main line. That year his daughter Eleanor inherited his entire estates in Durham and Cumbria. Eleanor married her kinsman, Sir William Tempest of Trafford (Durham) and Studley (Yorkshire). When she died a widow in 1452 the Washington estate included 200 acres and the site south of the church with 'hall, chambers and other houses' (attached buildings). Their only daughter Dionysia married Sir William Mallory.

Under non-resident sub-tenants in the 16th century the property declined steadily. Government Commissions, enquiring into decaying Border agriculture and defence, record that many tenancies here had decayed by 1584; and in 1593 Washington Hall, Sir William Mallory's property, had no resident 'footemen' (men-at-arms) although many were kept in 1535-6. The offending tenant was Robert Witherington who died in 1598.
The manor continued to be held by Wessyngton descendants until 1613 when the lease from the bishop was sold to trustees for William James, Bishop of Durham, who settled it on his youngest son Francis, then a minor aged 14.

The Later Washingtons

Meantime the Washington family had migrated to Lancashire and Cumbria. John de Wessyngton married Elizabeth, heiress of Gilbert de Burneside and acquired land near Kendal. Their eldest son Robert married Joan de Strickland of Sizergh Castle. From this line descended Lawrence Washington who was very successful in the wool trade, moving to Northamptonshire where he became Mayor of Northampton and bought Sulgrave manor where the family lived for many years. George Washington was descended from the Reverend Lawrence Washington who was born at Sulgrave in 1602, but was deprived of his living because of his loyalty to the Royalist cause in the mid-17th century. His son John became a merchant and emigrated to America in 1656 and, with his brother Lawrence, settled in Virginia. His great-grandson was George Washington.

The 17th Century

At Washington, the Hall was partly demolished and rebuilt in its present form about 1623 for Francis James. His son William James lived there from his marriage in 1645 until his death on 5 April 1662. His widow Dorothy, a benefactor to the church, continued to live here. Their only son, William, died in 1663, leaving his four sisters as co-heiresses. Through descendants of their marriages, Washington was eventually divided between three families: Lawson, Musgrave and Shafto. Dorothy was married a second time to the Reverend Ralph Maddison, an un-beneficed clergyman who died in 1700. The Hall was held jointly and after the death of Dorothy James in 1701, was let to tenants. In the 18th century the most important of these were the Bracks. James Brack died in 1784 and on completion of alterations to the Hall, his successor John Brack placed a sundial (since perished), dated 1792, on the south face of the stair turret, which had been added to an H-shaped house of the 'hall and ends' pattern.

The main door was on the north side which retains its symmetrical appearance and faces the church. The outline of a projecting portico can be traced on the existing stone work. The present north door was the inner door, which has a deep socket on either side to carry a heavy wooden bar.

Under later tenants the Hall was divided and occupied as tenements. Part of the land on the south, which had formed the courtyard, was sold off. The Hall was put on the market as unfit for human habitation. When its importance was recognised, it was saved from demolition by a Preservation Committee in 1936 which restored and furnished it, with generous help from both sides of the Atlantic. In 1955 it was opened by the American ambassador and two years later handed over to the National Trust.

During restoration features from the original house were found embedded in the 17th-century house. At the west end of the hall two arches were unblocked and restored. One had been partly demolished and partly blocked to insert a doorway with oak jambs. These arches were found behind a modern brick chimney breast. They led into the kitchen quarters from a screens passage formed by a wooden partition across this end of the hall to a door to the south leading to domestic offices. The open kitchen fireplace, with roasting jacks and spits, is a 17th-century introduction; but on the right is part of one of the windows of the original house, a deeply splayed opening with an arched head. Between this and the fireplace is another medieval window with an oak frame and mullions. It appears that the original window was blocked to make room for the second, and this in its turn was partially blocked to admit the right-hand jamb of the fireplace. Most of the walls of the present kitchen were survivals of the original manor house. The original hall has left no trace of the dais at the west end where the owner would have dined. The original fireplace here had been replaced by a kitchen range when the house was converted into tenements. The present early 17th-century fireplace, with swords and a heart carved on the head, came from Newburn Manor on the Tyne, now demolished. At the east end is the withdrawing room, or private room of

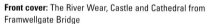

Beamish, North of England Open Air Museum: colliery village main street

the medieval owner. The present fine Jacobean panelling came from the Old Manor House, Abbots Langley, presented by Miss Mabel Choate in memory of her father, the American Ambassador to Britain. She also gave the other furnishings in the room. The fireplace is original.

The fine 17th-century staircase, from the White Hart Hotel, Guildford, was presented by Lord and Lady Gort to replace the original which was burnt out long ago. Upstairs are three rooms, formerly six, with original fireplaces. One is set out as a 17th-century bedroom. The main room is used as a community centre for Washington people.

Miss Choate also had the upper garden laid out as a memorial to Eric Underwood, who did much to promote Anglo-American relationships.

The lower garden to the south was recently extended to enclose land, formerly part of the medieval courtyard, recovered by the Friends of the Old Hall and from 2003 planted as a nuttery with pleasant walks.

The present entrance is from The Avenue on the west, a road made in 1831. The 18th-century entrance gates were presented by Chapter XI of the Colonial Dames of America. The adjacent 17th-century cottage was probably the 'bothy', reconstructed at the expense of Charles Sumner Bird, of Walpole, Massachusetts.

The **Washington Wildfowl and Wetlands Centre** on the north bank of the River Wear has hundreds of ducks, geese, swans and flamingos, besides a large colony of grey herons, and a developing colony of the common tern.

There is a waterfowl nursery and a café. (For details of opening times and directions telephone 0191 416 5454 or visit www.washington@wwf.org.uk).

Beamish: North of England Open Air Museum

Beamish is on the A693, signposted from the A1 (M) Chester-le-Street exit, junction 63. The site covers 200 acres of beautiful County Durham countryside, and vividly illustrates life in the North of England in the early 1800s and 1900s. It has a drift mine, colliery village, home farm with traditional breeds of animals and poultry, railway station with rolling stock and signal box, a Methodist chapel, and a school. At Pockerley Manor, the lifestyle of a yeoman family almost 200 years ago is recreated. Visitors take a tram ride to visit the town with its shops, working pub, stables, garage, newspaper office, sweet factory, dentist and other professional houses.

Beamish has won the distinction of being British Museum of the Year and European Museum of the Year.

There is much else to do and see in the area. Contact the Tourist Information Office, Millennium Place for other places to visit, times of opening, and admission charges where applicable.

Front cover: The River Wear, Castle and Cathedral from Framwellgate Bridge
Back cover: Neptune, replaced from Wharton Park in 1991, surmounted the Market Place pant or well from 1729 to 1920.

Visitors should ask Tourist Information for times of opening, as they change according to season.
First published, 1970 Second edition, 1974
Third edition, revised and rearranged with additions, 1982
Fourth edition, with colour photographs, 1983
Fifth edition, revised and with additions, 1987
Sixth edition, revised and with additions, 1992
Seventh edition, revised, with additions and new photographs, 1997
The text, newly revised and with additions, was previously published as *Durham: a pictorial history and guide.*
© Margot Johnson, 1970, 1974, 1982, 1983, 1987, 1992, 1997
Acknowledgements
All photographs supplied and © as follows:
Peter Ryder for illustration of a Brancepeth cross slab and valuable contribution on Brancepeth church archaeology.
Jonathan Gough for pictures of South Street, Collingwood College, St Mary's College and College coats of arms, St Cuthbert's Society, St John's College, St Chad's College, Grey College, Hatfield College, Trevelyan College.
National Trust for pictures of Washington Old Hall.
University of Durham for picture of Botanic Garden.
St Aidan's College for picture of the College.
All other pictures © Jarrold Publishing and Margot Johnson.

Designed and produced by Jarrold Publishing.
Text by Margot Johnson.
Project Manager: John Armitage Design: Kaarin Wall
Printed in Great Britain. Jarrold Publishing 1/04 ISBN 0946105 16 2
www.jarrold-publishing.co.uk